The Little Book Of

COCAINE

Printed and bound in the UK by MPG Books, Bodmin

Distributed in the US by Publishers Group West

Published by Sanctuary Publishing Limited, Sanctuary House, 45-53 Sinclair
Road, London W14 0NS, United Kingdom

www.sanctuarypublishing.com

Cover photo: © Getty Images
Reprinted 2004

ISBN: 1-86074-526-1

The Little Book Of

COCAINE

Nick Constable

Sanctuary

CONTENTS

INTRODUCTION

There's someone you've got to meet. His name's Charlie and he gets to go to all the best parties. He's the club king of London and New York, mixes with pop stars and celebrities, has loads of contacts on Wall Street and is just about everyone's best friend in TV land. When Charlie's around you feel like a million dollars and when he leaves it's such a let-down. He's totally cool. Just treat him with a little respect.

Respect is about right. Around the world cocaine is more accessible than ever, and yet the social and scientific arguments swirling around it seem to get denser by the year. Coke is not the kind of drug you place in a tidy little box, because everything about it defies simple analysis. Suffice to say that it is a substance of contradiction: of euphoria and despair; of obscene wealth and dire poverty. It knows no social barriers. Use it wisely and you'll be fine. Or maybe not.

CHARLIE'S FRIENDS

We're talking about the champagne drug of celebrities, yet loads of addicts are beggars and prostitutes. Its chemistry sustains Peruvian hill farmers just as much as sharp-suited banking professionals. You can be an occasional snorter for years and not have a problem but get psychologically hooked with surprising speed if you smoke it. Some say the drug guarantees great sex, others just want to re-organize their mantelpiece. You'll sell a line to your best friend with a clear conscience, yet you know, deep down, that you've joined an industry that maims and kills to protect its markets.

By the way, got any cocaine on you? Bet you have. It may be that the only white powder looming large in your life comes from the vending machine at your local launderette, but Charlie gets everywhere. Especially into your purse or wallet.

HE'S A POPULAR GUY

In 1999, a BBC survey conducted by the forensic chemists Mass Spec Analytical discovered that out of 500 banknotes circulating in London, 99 per cent carried traces of cocaine. About 1 in 20 produced a particularly high reading, suggesting they had been used to snort it. The rest had probably been contaminated during handling by users and dealers.

Joe Reevy of Mass Spec explained, 'Once you've taken a snort, the compounds will be in the oils of your skin and they'll get transferred to the notes you handle. That's the main way in which the cocaine gets on to the notes. When you test notes that have been used directly to snort cocaine you get a great big reading and the machine takes quite a while to settle down. You don't miss the difference.'

This study came less than a month after the government-backed British crime survey concluded that cocaine was the fastest-growing recreational drug among 20- to 24- year-olds. Two years later, in April 2001, *The Face* magazine published a survey of 1,000 16- to 24- year-olds, which showed that more than half of those questioned had taken it. *The Face* editor Johnny Davis said prices as low as £10 ($14) per gram (that really is bargain-basement stuff) had attracted this new custom.

'Our suspicion, borne out by the findings, is that cocaine users are younger and more varied than ever before,' he said. 'A glamour drug that was once a celebrity and media choice has become cheaper and more accessible.' Mike Goodman, director of the UK drugs advice line Release agreed, pointing out that clubs where cocaine was popular also did a roaring trade in champagne. 'It's all linked to lifestyle,' he said. 'People have got more money, cocaine is cheaper. You can get it for £40 [$60] a gram, which people will club together and buy to share between them on a Saturday night.'

The UN's *Global Illicit Drug Trends* report for 2001 confirms a rising trend in western Europe, South and Central America, South Africa and Australia. What is termed 'occasional' cocaine use has stabilized in the USA (the world's largest market) at 1.7 per cent of the population aged 12 and over. This is a reduction of two-thirds on the 1985 level. Even so, when 'hardcore' (ie at least weekly) users are counted there are currently 6.6 million people, or 3 per cent of the entire US population, who take cocaine. Spin the numbers however you will; this is not a drug bound for oblivion.

CHARLIE: A POTTED BIOGRAPHY

So where and why do people take cocaine? How can cocaine culture be defined in the 21st century? To break down the big picture, it's worth separating South American chewers (coca leaf) from snorters (powder coke), smokers (crack cocaine or 'freebase'), mainliners (injected coke solution) and drinkers (usually coke dissolved in alcohol). For reasons that will become clear, it's the chewers and snorters who mostly get along without setting up home in the gutter. Mainliners and drinkers are rarer breeds and are probably flirting with trouble. Regular crack smokers generally claim they're not addicted. Generally, they're lying.

CHEWERS AND SNORTERS

Coca leaf chewing has been going on for thousands of years in South America and only very rarely causes social or health problems. Powder coke has been around in the West for about 120 years and doesn't necessarily affect a user's health. That's not to say it is either safe or harmless. If you've got the money and the lifestyle that allow you to snort ten lines a day (a line is about one-twentieth of a gram or two-hundredths of an ounce) you're fast-tracking towards a serious habit. But a lot of users don't do cocaine this way. They'll take a line or two at a party or during a night out clubbing, and they won't touch it during the week. This is one reason why comparatively few coke and ecstasy users end up in hospital emergency departments.

SMOKERS

Freebase and crack cocaine are more recent derivatives of the drug and those that plan to fish in these waters need to be much more careful. When a drug is smoked, it reaches the brain in under four seconds. Recent research suggests that this speed of delivery greatly boosts cocaine's addictive qualities and leads to the 'bingeing' so common among crack and freebase addicts.

WHO IS THIS BOOK FOR?

This book is for users, their friends and parents, and anyone interested in a balanced perspective of cocaine in today's world. It looks at the drug's curious history, its links with music and showbusiness, fashion and pop culture. It explores the extraordinary underworld dealings of drug lords, traffickers and smugglers, and explains why crack has emerged as a key factor in street crime and gang warfare. It considers the power politics that drive world coca-leaf production, and the terrible poverty that afflicts either end of the trade, from growers to consumers. Above all, it explains the science of cocaine addiction, the health implications and ways in which users can minimize risk.

If you're doing cocaine, or you know someone who is, then it's worth taking a look.

SOMETHING FOR THE WEEKEND?

For the best part of a century cocaine has been the music lover's drug of choice. The link dates back to the early American jazz and blues scene but it re-emerged strongly in popular culture with the *Easy Rider* generation of the late 1960s, the fast-living rockers of the 1970s and the new romantics of the 1980s. More recently, it has permeated clubland where, though ecstasy remains the market leader, a core of older clubbers see coke as more sophisticated and manageable.

With a rush lasting barely 40 minutes, party lovers know they can pep themselves up on the dance floor and come down whenever they need to resume normal service. As one regular user of both drugs explained, 'With ecstasy you spend 15 hours grinning at everyone. With C [coke] you can buy a £20 [$30] half-gram special and just dip in and out of your emotions.'

Ed Jaram, editor of the British-based Internet club magazine *Spaced*, says that price is also a factor in the drug divide among the country's 1.5 million regular clubbers.

'There is some resistance to powder coke on the scene,' he says. 'First, it's more expensive and so tends to be used by an older, more affluent crowd. Second, clubbers want to know what they're buying. With pills you can see a stamp and you pretty much know what you've got. But with coke you could be buying speed or even talcum powder. You don't know until you try it.

'As a currency in clubs I don't think coke will ever overtake ecstasy, although a lot of people are starting to combine the two. For sure, everyone on the dance floor looks like they've been fuelled by the same ecstasy dealer but, chances are, there'll be quite a few older clubbers in there using coke or taking it cocktail style with Es.'

CLUBBERS' DELIGHT
London is the unchallenged club capital of Britain and club nights are essentially multimedia fashion statements. And, of course, drugs are part of this show, despite the body searches on the door and the official warning words from police and proprietors.

'Cocaine and ecstasy use is now so widespread, and so accepted by promoters and the police, that the legal position isn't much of a talking point,' says Jaram. 'Everyone has their own view but it is taken for granted in Britain that you can go to a club and do drugs and nobody is going to mind.

'Promoters and owners are very, very tolerant towards this lifestyle. You can buy your stuff, take it in and do it, and you know you're not going to get thrown out. The question of legalization doesn't arise because you're using drugs anyway without hassle.

'As a general rule clubbers are aware of the dangers they face. This is much more important to them than whether some politician somewhere says a drug is legal or not. There certainly isn't the kind of repression found in, say, New York, where clubs are influenced by a zero-tolerance attitude to anything perceived as crime.'

REDUCING THE RISKS?
This may be true, although the British government is beaming out some confused signals. In March 2002 the Home Office launched a booklet entitled *Safer Clubbing*. This called for more effort to stop weapons being smuggled past doormen but also acknowledged that coke and ecstasy were part of the club scene. The booklet urged proprietors to provide more drinking water, cut out overcrowding and overheating, improve ventilation, train staff to spot the effects of intoxication and offer a 'calm environment' where users can chill out or get treatment.

'If we cannot stop them from taking drugs then we must be prepared to take steps to reduce the harm that they may cause themselves,' said Bob Ainsworth, Home Office minister.

This is fine and dandy, except the Home Office also announced proposals for tough new laws aimed at jailing proprietors and nightclub managers who knowingly allow 'dance-scene' drugs like cocaine to be consumed on their premises. At the very least, this is a contradiction in policy. The message to clubs is: 'Keep drug users safe when they're on your premises. And by the way, don't let them in at all.'

A REAL GROWTH INDUSTRY

According to a Home Office study published in 2001 – *Middle Market Drug Distribution*, by Geoffrey Pearson (Goldsmiths College) and Dick Hobbs (University of London) – the clubbing scene is 'a modern system of fraternity that can facilitate drug networks and highly accelerated drug dealing careers'. Pearson and Hobbs interviewed prisoners who started by selling a few tablets around the dance scene and progressed within months to become 'serious middle market drugs brokers'.

One 21-year-old woman told them: 'Once I started, other people got to hear, and that type of thing, it escalates very quickly... I was on the club scene every week, meeting different people, socializing. People come saying, "Can you get me some?" And as soon as it started – phew! – it got out of control, really.'

A 30-year-old man explained how in a typical weekend he would shift 2,500 ecstasy pills, 4kg (9lb) of marijuana, 110g (4oz) of cocaine and various quantities of speed and LSD. He started selling to friends, then friends of friends and a network quickly built up. 'Eventually you've got other people who want to start dealing and then dealers buy from you and it's a sky rocket before you even know it. I don't agree with selling in clubs, it's more like pushing drugs... I didn't push drugs at all. I did a social thing for friends and then it just got bigger.'

Networking is the lifeblood of the cocaine dealer. The sharper ones will sell you a few lines and then invite you to a party to share them. If you run out – no problem: there's plenty more for sale.

AMERICA ONLINE

London's bar and club cocaine culture is rarely troubled by the law. Police busts aimed at users (as opposed to dealers) are rare. However, across the pond in New York there is a much more repressive attitude towards recreational drugs, so far with little deterrent effect. One correspondent working in the Big Apple for a British national newspaper during the 1990s described cocaine as 'the ultimate night-out accessory'. He was not a user but came to regard it as no different to alcohol and tobacco. 'In some ways it's more socially acceptable than both,' he says. 'You get it in little white home-made envelopes, which somehow seems a nice personal touch.

'It can be a pretty undignified method of consumption – bending over a bog seat and sniffing – but once that's out of the way then the result is attractive. Cocaine doesn't poison other people, like tobacco smoke, and it doesn't make your drinking companion vomit 12 lagers over you.

If you're a club regular, or a stock trader, or in the media, then coke comes with the territory. The police keep publicizing these big drugs clampdowns but most New Yorkers on the scene don't even notice. If anything, cocaine is getting easier to buy.'

Today, corporate America remains awash with the drug. There's a dealers' paradise on South Beach, Miami, Florida, every March, when thousands of house-, techno- and electronic-music fans descend for the annual Winter Music Conference. This is supposed to unearth strange new beats and cutting-edge artists, but more recently it has become an exercise in branding, marketing and corporate focus groups. Where full-on music company executives meet the house crowd you can bet your deck blender that cocaine supplies will be somewhere nearby. Usually in a large truck.

Cocaine powers the music business – not just the dance scene – and has done for much of the 20th century. When in 2001 the British rock music TV channel VH1 ran a poster advertising campaign, it used a photo of three children's drinking straws alongside a rolled-up banknote apparently tipped with white powder. The copy read: 'VH1. Music TV that's not for kids.'

MUSIC, FASHION, WORK...AND A LINE FOR CELEBRITIES
In 1975, the American rock legend JJ Cale wrote the song 'Cocaine'. It's inconceivable that you don't know the lyrics but here's a brief reminder anyway:

If you wanna hang out you've got to take her out - cocaine
If you wanna get down, down on the ground - cocaine
She don't lie, she don't lie, she don't lie - cocaine

The song became an anthem for the cocaine boom of the 1970s and reinforced the tabloid press view that all filthy-rotten-rich rock stars were on the stuff. As generalizations go, this one was on the button. It didn't apply so much to the punk movement mind, because punks saw cocaine as a bourgeois affectation, completely unnecessary when you could pop speed and ecstasy.

Still, over the last three decades, your typical pop star seems to have been at least an occasional coke-head. Songs like Black Sabbath's 'Snowblind' or Suede's 'We Are The Pigs', the latter written after an experience of coke-induced paranoia according to the band's Brett Anderson, kept cocaine up there as a fashion drug.

CHARLIE'S WITH THE BAND...

You get up in the morning, surrounded by empty bottles,
and the mirror's covered in smears of cocaine and the
first thing you do is lick the mirror – Elton John recalling
the drug days of his early career in the 1970s (according
to John's biographer Philip Norman the singer got such
a megalomanic buzz from the drug that he once asked
aides to 'turn down the wind' because the sound of
swaying trees was bothering him)

Cocaine is a very spiteful bedfellow. If you want to lose all the friends and relationships you ever held dear, that's the drug to do it with - David Bowie, in his 'Thin White Duke' phase

I take cocaine. Big fucking deal - Noel Gallagher, Oasis

There's a fucking blizzard of cocaine in London at the moment and I hate it. It's stupid. Everyone's become so blasé, thinking they're so ironic and witty and wandering around with that stupid fucking cokey confidence. Wankers. I did it, but I can't say I was a cocaine addict - Damon Albarn, Blur, speaking in 1996

By the time I was 23 I was addicted but it didn't seem to matter in our business. No one thought it was unusual to be up all night doing lines of coke - Alan McGee, head of Creation Records

As you can see, cocaine was - and still is - ingrained in music culture. Sir Paul McCartney tried it when he was writing The Beatles *Sgt Pepper's Lonely Hearts Club Band* album in 1966. He got the drug from art gallery dealer Robert Fraser (one of the bastions of trendy London in the 1960s), who was, in turn, supplied by an American designer. In a biography entitled *Groovy Bob*, Harriet Vyner tells how Fraser also introduced The Rolling Stones to coke, along with a beautiful young member of their circle called Marianne Faithfull.

Apparently when Marianne was offered her first line she didn't know the etiquette and snorted in one go everything that Fraser had laid out. At least she didn't go the way of lead guitarist Ronnie Wood, widely reported to have destroyed part of his nose through overuse of the drug. It was said that Wood woke up one morning to discover that he could see the bathroom sink through the top of his hooter.

During the 1970s, when rock 'n' roll excesses were attaining new heights, rumours circulated about a new method of taking cocaine that wouldn't give you a rotten proboscis. The drug can be absorbed into the blood through any membrane (this is why it's sometimes rubbed on gums) and, inevitably, imaginative types explored a variety of techniques. Apparently the rock stars' 'special' involved anal administration, colloquially known as gak blowing, and gossip abounded about bands with a resident gak blower on their tour bus.

Doing cocaine is now practically expected in the music business. We're not quite at the point where record-company executives give superstars a roasting on the grounds that they should snort – or perhaps gak – more lines, but it can't be far off. Just look at Robbie Williams, for whom coke has arguably been career enhancing.

During his years with Take That, Williams signed up to the scrupulously controlled sparkly clean image demanded by record-label bosses. Then in June 1995 he threw his toys out of his cot and headed for the Glastonbury rock festival with Oasis. As he later told music magazine *Select*, he tried 'every drug except heroin'. Since then, Williams has deservedly achieved superstar status – both for his songwriting and singing. As quickly as he took up his bad-boy image he dumped it, attending a rehab centre, slimming down and staying clean of drugs.

COKE ON THE CATWALK

Cocaine was, at the same time, becoming the unspoken accessory of fashion modelling. There are obvious reasons for this. Like pop stars, models need to keep a good handle on their image. You can't shimmy down a catwalk with puncture marks in your arms or a big gurney grin shaped by too much ecstasy the night before. You can't be drunk because it's not conducive to moving in straight lines. Amphetamines are out because, hell, you'd do the catwalk in a personal best of 7.2 seconds. What you need is a drug that gets your eyes sparkling (by restricting the blood supply to them) and your confidence zooming. Just a little make-up for the mind.

Naomi Campbell tried to sue the London-based *Mirror* newspaper for compensation after it revealed that she was receiving therapy for drug abuse and had attended Narcotics Anonymous meetings. Campbell won rather a pyrrhic victory, receiving only £3,500 ($5,070) on a somewhat technical legal argument. She was also accused by the High Court judge of lying under oath.

The evidence was, as always in these cases, much more interesting than the outcome. In a written statement, *Mirror* editor Piers Morgan argued that publication was justified because Campbell had publicly denied her addiction to drugs while committing a serious offence 'by possessing and using a Class A drug – cocaine – over a period of years'.

The Californian-born icon Carre Otis, who in the 1990s became the face of Calvin Klein, admitted in a 2002 interview with the London *Sunday Times* that she used the drug to help maintain her skeletal figure. She is now clean and an attractively healthy 'plus-size' (as they euphemistically term it in the clothes-horse business).

'The only way that I have ever been a size 10 was when I starved myself,' she said. 'Or I was doing huge amounts of cocaine or just drinking and not eating. That's the only time I have ever been really skinny.' For Otis, use of the drug carried a terrible history. Aged just 15 she had been dating the son of a Californian politician when the boy lost a soccer match, got himself high on cocaine and blew his brains out. The suicide note was addressed to her.

THE SOCIALITE'S CHUM

In fact, as she later realised, cocaine was the controller of the pain. This was also the experience of queen of the 'It' Girls, Tara Palmer-Tomkinson, who in 1990s Britain became the darling of the popular press – proper posh totty according to the red-top papers. Palmer-Tomkinson's forte was partying and being outrageous – that and the fact that her family knew Prince Charles very well.

In an article for the *Daily Mail*'s Weekend magazine in 2002 she wrote: 'As an It Girl it was simply my job to amuse. I took the role very seriously. I always tried to entertain: to sing for my supper. And sadly, this is how I started to rely on cocaine.

'...It seemed to give me the energy and the confidence I needed to discourse brilliantly with people from all walks of life. To begin with, I took it before an evening out but the habit escalated and soon I couldn't face the world without it. At the same time I realised that the confidence it gave me was illusory. Cocaine began to eat away at my self-esteem. It took away my natural vivacity and made me restless and paranoid. I was still going to three parties a night and I could never sit still.'

She tried to fight this by returning regularly to the family home in Hampshire for drug-free recuperation. But when she got back to London she got back to cocaine.

ACTING UP
It was the kind of self-deceptive nightmare succinctly summed up by American actor/director and one-time three-grams-a-day coke user Dennis Hopper. Even when he stopped drinking in 1983 and began attending Alcoholics

Anonymous, it took him another year to finally kiss goodbye to cocaine.

'I would turn up at meetings, saying "I'm an alcoholic" with half an ounce of cocaine in my pocket,' he told the London *Daily Telegraph* in 2001. 'And I wouldn't smoke grass, or use any downers or anything because that was going to take me over the edge. I mean, how crazy am I? So, finally, I just burned out again, and the radio was talking to me and the electric wires – boy, I was out of it. So if anybody has any doubts about cocaine – cocaine is just as bad on its own without any help from anything else.'

SNOW ON THE SMALL SCREEN

The *EastEnders* soap actress Danniella Westbrook was less fortunate. Little known outside the UK, her cocaine habit produced a powerful reminder of how heavy use of the drug can break down human tissue. Photographs of her taken during 2000 showed how her septum (the part of her nose between the nostrils) had vanished, her single nasal orifice a cruel parody of the star's former beauty. This is a condition that can be rectified by plastic surgery, but it shattered her career – at least temporarily.

Westbrook's rumoured £300-a-day ($435) habit revealed an astonishing level of addiction for a woman still in her mid-20s and is untypical of most users. As the journalist and author Julie Burchill put it later: 'I just don't know how she did it. Between 1986 and 1996 I must have put enough toot up my admittedly sizeable snout to stun the entire Colombian armed forces and still it sits there, Romanesque and proud, all too bloody solid actually.'

Other British celebrities have lived to regret cocaine's allure for different reasons. John Alford, a star of the hit TV fire service drama *London's Burning*, was jailed for nine months and lost his £120,000-a-year ($175,000) role after he was caught selling the drug to an undercover reporter. It took four years for him to claw his way back into a minor TV role. But the biggest scandal to hit British television came in March 2001 when Stuart Lubbock, a party guest at the Essex home of TV presenter and comedian Michael Barrymore, was found dead in the star's swimming pool.

In a TV interview with the journalist Martin Bashir, Barrymore denied allegations that he had given cocaine to his guests and said he had merely smoked cannabis on the night, but he also admitted: 'Any time I wasn't working I would immediately start drinking and taking pills just to get me away. I took drugs as well. I smoked pot, [took] cocaine, Es, speed, anything.' After a year-long investigation, Essex police announced that no further action would be taken. Barrymore escaped with an arrest and caution for possession of cannabis and allowing his home to be used for smoking the drug.

AMERICAN HIGH
America, though, remains the spiritual home of the cocaine scandal. Perhaps the best known involved the comedian

Richard Pryor, who on 9 June 1980 had just finished a freebase smoking binge (still a strange concept to most Americans) when he decided to round things off by drinking the high-percentage-proof rum swilling around his waterpipe. After five days non-stop freebasing Pryor was pretty much shot to shreds and he spilled the rum down his highly flammable nylon shirt. Then he decided to light a cigarette, ignited the fumes as well and effectively blew himself up. He needed months of burns treatment but was still able to joke to an audience how he 'did the 100-yard dash in 4.3'.

Pryor was lucky. Not so fellow comedian John Belushi. He was lured by the intrinsically dangerous 'speedball' cocktail of heroin and cocaine, an upper-downer combination that has fascinated habitual drug users for much of the 20th century. The two drugs combine extremely well in terms of their buzz, although the physical effect has been likened to driving at maximum revs with the brakes screaming. For Belushi, loved by millions as the anarchic star of the cult movie *The Blues Brothers*, it was one ride too many. He died in March 1982 of a speedball overdose.

STREET CRIME

Cocaine and crime are soulmates. Especially in western cities. Nowhere is this more true than London, which in 2001 saw an explosion in inter-gang violence and street crime apparently caused by crack addicts desperate for some rocks. The major crack suppliers in Britain are Jamaican or of Jamaican origin: often described as 'Yardie' gangs. They have Caribbean associates who arrange imports from Colombia while they act as wholesalers in overall control of UK and some European distribution. They are part of a worldwide trafficking operation. They may also organize street dealing and sales to approved dealers.

According to the head of Scotland Yard's Flying Squad, Commander Alan Brown, Yardie-style gangsters are now the most violent and difficult criminals faced by British police. On 16 January 2002 he released figures showing 21 drug-related murders and 67 attempted murders in London the previous year. All but two of the capital's 32 boroughs (districts) had reported drug-linked crime and all but ten had seen shootings. In the previous fortnight police had logged the first two murders of the new year and a further 25 shootings. All of this was 'black-on-black' crime.

The figures for gun crime across England and Wales rose by 9 per cent in 2001 to 4,019 incidents. It's hard to know how much of this was linked to cocaine in particular and drugs in general, but police believe that a significant proportion is down to Yardie in-fighting and feuding. It is all uncannily similar to the extreme violence on the streets of Miami and New York in the 1980s when America woke up to its own crack epidemic.

PSYCHIATRIC TOXICITY?

While London's crack cocaine gangs are not necessarily drug users themselves they certainly seem to be mad about guns. At Scotland Yard, Alan Brown heads the Operation Trident task force, which targets the big players. He has cited specific instances of how easily shootings are provoked in disputes about drugs, territory or 'respect'. Examples include:

- a sarcastic remark made by one black gangster about another's hairstyle
- a man treading on a gang leader's foot by mistake in a nightclub
- a nightclub bouncer refusing entry to a gang enforcer; the man returned with a gun and sprayed bullets at a queue waiting to enter the club; eight people were injured
- a row between a party-goer and a DJ in which the DJ was shot dead; the bullet passed through a wall, killing a second man.

'There are clearly organizations in both Jamaica and [the UK] that have almost a business relationship for supply and retail,' said Brown. 'The drug and gun culture is producing an incredibly narcissistic generation of young criminals. Their reaction to any act of what they see as disrespect is extreme violence.'

TRAFFICK ISLAND

According to Jamaican police there were around 500 known criminals from the island operating in Britain in 2002. The majority are affiliated to some 30 Yardie gangs: organizations with imaginative names such as the Kickoffhead Crew, the Lock City Crew, the Cartel Crew, the African Crew, the British Link Up Crew, Clans Massive, the Black Roses and the President's Click. The Click was apparently formed out of the notorious Shower Posse gang, rumoured to have committed 1,400 murders in the USA.

Just like the New York and Chicago gangsters of the 1920s and 1930s the Jamaican networks began life as election 'muscle', bullies hired to ensure that voters would support either the left-wing People's National Party or the conservative Jamaican Labour Party. Whereas Al Capone and his Chicago associates got rich on bootlegged alcohol, the Yardie leaders realised that cocaine was their ticket to riches. On 10 February 2002 the London-based *Sunday Times* named the leader of the President's Click and quoted a Jamaican police officer as saying: 'He is wanted for everything: murder, drug running, you name it. He is linked to gangs in the UK but he is untouchable because of his political links. That is the culture in Jamaica.'

DEALING WITH IT

British police have responded to the cocaine crimewave. Brown's Operation Trident arrested 441 people in 2001, most aged between 16 and 35. Of the 620 kilos of Class A drugs recovered nearly all was cocaine. Similar operations are ongoing: 'Stirrup' in Leeds, which resulted in 57 deportations to Jamaica in 2001; 'Atrium' in Bristol; 'Ventara' in Birmingham; 'Trojan' in Southampton; and 'Ovidian' in Plymouth.

Although Britain's crack market is Jamaican-controlled there is no evidence that the drug is used mostly in black communities. According to one senior Metropolitan Police detective it has penetrated all social backgrounds, with a 'heartland' of users – mostly beggars – in Soho, central London. This officer, a member of the London Crime Squad, heads an undercover team that buys crack on the street, busts key players and passes intelligence to other units. He has 21 years' experience, the past four in drugs operations.

'There is no great class divide,' he told me. 'Crack cocaine is used by all racial groups although beggars are the big market. If you go to black areas like Brixton you will obviously tend to find more black users. The same is true for white areas – particularly, in outer south-east London. There are several nightclubs where it is used by the black community but crack is not a club drug in the same league as, say, ecstasy.

'In areas of the West End, particularly around Soho, the customers are pretty much all vagrants. These are people who will beg for a quantity of pound coins until they have enough money to buy a stone. There is also a significant passing trade in office workers – men and women in suits – both black and white people.

The Metropolitan Police anti-crack team pays maybe £20 (about $30) a stone (a piece of crack cocaine), which typically weighs about 200mg. Stones fluctuate from 50–60g (1¾–2oz) to around 300g (10½oz) and, like powder coke, they will have varying levels of purity depending on the recipe used to cook them. Maintaining a crack habit without a healthy income or resorting to prostitution is nigh on impossible, however good your sob story to passers-by.

'People talk glibly about smoking a dozen stones a day,' said the detective. 'That means the drug is costing them perhaps £200 ($290) daily, and although there's a discount if they buy in bulk, crime is often the only way to pay. Users become desperate for crack and will do almost anything to get it. This may mean robbing someone in the street, especially if they need a stone urgently and haven't the means of finding money quickly. In the last four years crack crime has been a constant problem and it has escalated in that time.

'There's no such thing as a typical street dealer, but there are very few that have full-time jobs. We did find somebody who worked at a hairdresser's shop in the morning and then cruised the streets selling cocaine in the afternoon. Dealers basically work the hours they want to.

'Some sell straight to the crack houses. There are a plethora of these in London, addresses where users know they can go to smoke out of sight. It is a huge problem but it is almost impossible to estimate the total number of users. From our experience I would say the majority are aged under 30.'

He believes the fight against crack dealing is not hopeless, but demands a rolling review of police tactics. 'There is also an immigration issue here with carriers entering the UK, particularly from Jamaica,' he said. 'We need to look at these drug mules more closely and identify those who sponsor their application to enter Britain.'

Young, homeless, addicted, broke and desperate to service a craving for crack. No wonder cocaine has become synonymous with crime around the world. But if you think this is only a problem for the major cities think again. Crack dealers are businessmen. They thrive on making and defending new markets.

WHAT'S THE SET-UP?

Street dealers use a variety of business models. The most basic has a single trader buying and selling small quantities, often to fund his own habit. More usually (according to Pearson and Hobbs) there will be a team centred on a leader who buys wholesale and assigns runners to make street deliveries or take payments. This leader maintains the books and keeps the contacts hot. There may also be peripheral employees, eg purity testers, crack cooks and packagers.

The UK Home Office's New English and Welsh Arrestee Drug Abuse Monitoring programme (NEW-ADAM), published in 2000, looked at cocaine and crack purchases in two British cities: Nottingham and Sunderland. Of the 131-strong sample, 82 per cent bought in their local neighbourhood and 75 per cent made contact with their dealer via a pager or mobile phone. Two-thirds were given a collection point (usually in a residential street) while the remainder had it delivered to their door by a courier.

In America cocaine markets traditionally work on a credit system in which the drug is supplied up-front by wholesalers to street dealers. The dealer than pays up over an agreed timescale. In the UK this model is less typical; sometimes cash on delivery is demanded within a network and sometimes it isn't. Either way it makes sense to keep drug and cash runners separate. If there's a bust or a taxing it means there's less to lose.

Dealers who peddle only one type of drug are comparatively rare. Marijuana is an exception because it is seen as all but legal. Why would grass-only suppliers wish to jeopardize a good business by dabbling in a drug like coke, with all the additional hassle from police and rival operators that might bring? Often street dealers will buy from 'multi-commodity brokers' offering club drugs such as speed, ecstasy, powder coke and perhaps a little marijuana on the side. Finally, there is the crack and heroin market, seen as a class apart because it involves 'dirty' habits. Even dealers and traffickers have morals...but not all of them. The level of violence used to extract payments and warn off competitors has no comparison in the criminal underworld. This occurs mostly at international trafficking level, but sometimes also between rival gangs in an individual city. None of the players goes looking for trouble because it stirs up police interest and is generally bad for business. Usually it's the sign of an unstable, disrupted supply chain or a good old-fashioned turf war.

COKE AT WORK AND PLAY

To appreciate the forces that drive worldwide cocaine trafficking you first have to crunch statistics. Drugs breed statistics. So this next bit is for all those anoraks who feel comfortable knowing that in Guatemala the annual prevalence of cocaine abuse as a percentage of the population aged 15 or over in 1998 was 1.6 per cent (*Global Illicit Drug Trends*, United Nations, 2001).

The Vienna-based International Drug Control Programme (UNIDCP) is a mine of fascinating facts on cocaine. In 2001 it estimated that the drug was used by 0.3 per cent of the global population with more than 70 per cent of these consumers living in North or South America and 16 per cent in Europe. Abuse levels in North America were seven times the world average, while Asians and eastern Europeans were noticeably abstemious. The continental breakdown is shown in the table over the page.

NUMBER OF COCAINE USERS (MILLIONS) AS A PERCENTAGE OF POPULATION AGED 15+

	MILLIONS	% OF POPULATION AGED 15+
North America	7.0	2.20
South America	3.1	1.10
Oceania	0.2	0.90
Western Europe	2.2	0.70
Eastern Europe	0.1	0.04
Africa	1.3	0.30
Asia	0.2	0.01
Global	14	0.30

WORLD OF COCAINE

More important than the hard data is the trend in consumption levels. Here's what the GIDT report for 2001 has to say about the pattern of cocaine use around the world. Most of the statistics are two to three years old (it takes this long to collect, collate and publish them) and there is inevitably a variation in sampling methods.

THE AMERICAS

Annual cocaine use (ie taking at least once a year) has stabilized in North America at 1.7 per cent of the population aged 12 and above. This is one-third lower than in 1985, while the number of monthly users fell even more dramatically over the same timespan: from 3 per cent to 0.7 per cent.

One illuminating section of the GIDT report is the 'Use, Risk, Disapproval and Availability' survey 2000, which looks at attitudes to cocaine and crack among American schoolchildren. This showed that just over 4 per cent of twelfth-graders used cocaine powder (down from 10 per cent in 1987). Half of the sample group said they saw 'great risk' in using it once or twice (same as 1987), 85 per cent said they disapproved of using once or twice (same as 1987) and just over 40 per cent said it was easy to get hold of (down from 50 per cent in 1987).

For crack, the figures revealed that 2 per cent of twelfth-graders in the sample had used in the past year (half the 1987 figure). Just under 50 per cent thought there were great risks attached to occasional use (down from 60 per cent in 1987). Around 85 per cent disapproved of using once or twice (slight decline on 1987) and 40 per cent said it was easy to obtain (same as 1987).

On the whole, these figures look encouraging for the US government. However, the report points out that even with a projected decline to 5.5 million users by 2000, the USA will remain far and away the world's biggest coke market.

Elsewhere in the Americas cocaine use is mostly on the increase. Peru and Bolivia – the two biggest coca leaf producers – are notable exceptions. Surveys there show a decline in the number of people experimenting with the drug during the 1990s. Brazil, Argentina and Chile now have the highest percentage of 'lifetime prevalence' cocaine powder abusers outside the USA. In Argentina the percentage of annual users is 1.9 per cent and in Chile 1.3 per cent. Colombia – the 'home of cocaine' – appears to have stable abuse levels (1.6 per cent of the population are lifetime users), although this figure was recorded back in 1996.

EUROPE

Data shows that Europe's two biggest cocaine markets – the UK and Spain – have stabilized. In contrast there is increasing use in Germany, France, The Netherlands, Belgium, Denmark, Norway, Portugal, Cyprus and Turkey. Eastern European countries barely perceive it as a problem. 'Cocaine in Europe – similar to the USA in the 1970s prior to the crack epidemic – is often used recreationally and constitutes less of a social problem than in North America,' says the report.

'However, there has been a trend towards poly-drug abuse ... many heroin addicts consume cocaine, increasingly in the form of crack. Similarly, there have been reports across western Europe of people on methadone maintenance programmes using cocaine to get their "kick".'

Another insight comes from the Brussels liaison department of the United Nations Office of Drug Control and Crime Prevention (UNODCCP). In 2001 it was generally upbeat about the trend in Europe. 'There was an increase in cocaine trafficking and consumption in Europe over the last decade – and this upward trend is probably going to continue. But it has been a creeping increase and there are no indications that this trend is likely to change dramatically in the near future. There are reports of youths who used to take ecstasy changing over to cocaine and there are reports of cocaine spreading from the upper class (or upper middle class) to other sections of society. But all of these trends do not appear – at least for the time being – to result in what could be called a cocaine epidemic.'

The UNODCCP also points out how the political history of a country can significantly affect consumption. In western Germany the number of people taking cocaine at least annually amounted to 0.7 per cent of the population in 1997, whereas in the eastern part of the country, the 'closed' provinces formerly under a communist regime reported a total of just 0.1 per cent. Presumably the Berlin Wall was a bummer for traffickers. Similarly, 'Only Spain, which has traditionally close links with its former colonies in Latin America, including the Andean region, has abuse levels of cocaine which approach those of the USA.' Spain's annual prevalence figure in 1997 was 1.5 per cent of the 15–65 age group.

The UNODCCP report concludes that 'Cocaine use in Europe is already widespread among people in entertainment, in the media and communications and some groups of professionals. There are no indications that the spread of cocaine among these sections of society is on the rise – they are rather ageing while using cocaine. Social security institutions may have to pay in one way or another for the resulting health problems. But use within these circles does not necessarily lead to a spread as members – usually – do not make their living out of drug trafficking.

'If there is an increase in cocaine use it could be expected to arise primarily among ageing groups of the "ecstasy generation" who may try to experiment with other drugs as well, including cocaine. But these groups – though representing potential health problems for themselves and for society at large – are at least less prone to undergo cocaine-related criminal activities than deprived youths living in some ghettos.'

AFRICA AND ASIA

The GIDT report reveals that cocaine abuse is largely a southern and western Africa phenomena. From the figures available there is increasing use in the Republic of South Africa and, especially, Angola (reflecting trafficking links with Brazil). Most cocaine shipped to Africa is intended for a final destination in Europe. Asian governments regard cocaine as a low-priority social issue. In 1999 only seven countries bothered to report trends in consumption and most of these were stable or falling.

OCEANIA

Australia is facing one of the biggest rises in cocaine abuse. The number of annual users almost tripled between 1993 and 1998 (from 0.5 per cent to 1.4 per cent of the population aged 14 and above), equivalent to the highest national rates found in Europe. This trend has not permeated to New Zealand, where year-on-year consumption is said to be stable.

PURER EQUALS MORE

One good indicator of coke availability can be found in the purity of police seizures. According to the 2001 GIDT report, 'As prices tend to remain rather stable in the drug markets, short-term changes in supply are usually reflected in shifts in purities. Higher levels of purities indicate improved supply.' In other words a street dealer with loads of Charlie on his hands doesn't worry too much about cutting. He passes on the improved quality to his buyers: just like any other customer-focused business.

The UNODCCP says that in 1999, mean cocaine purities exceeded 62 per cent in Britain. The last time purity levels topped this benchmark was in 1989 (it has ranged between 47 per cent and 55 per cent throughout the decade). While prosecution and seizure statistics will highlight bits of the story, most analysts agree that there's nothing like good old market forces to get to the nub of things. Cocaine powder 62 per cent pure is not a resounding victory for the forces of British law and order, and is a statistically significant change for the worse...or better, depending on your point of view.

GERMANY

Ah yes, Germany. The nation that first produced cocaine back in the 19th century has never quite ended its love affair with the drug. During the 1990s the decline in its street cocaine price was greater than anywhere else in Europe: it fell by two-thirds between 1996 and 1998. At Europe's busiest air hub, Frankfurt Airport, customs officers seized 780kg (1,720lbs) of the drug in 1995, compared to 421kg (925lbs) the previous year. In the first six months of 1999, according to the UNODCCP, 45 per cent of all cocaine seized in Germany was in transit to other European countries.

In fact, the 1997 report of Geopolitical Drug Watch (you're right, it could only be funded by the European Commission) revealed that cocaine dealing in Germany 'has broken out of its closed circle of distributors and consumers and has taken on the same mass character as heroin dealing. Those arrested include Nigerians, Italians, South Americans and eastern European nationals, but most were Germans; this diversity clearly demonstrates the splintering and democratization of the market.'

Democracy and cocaine is something the Bundestag knows all about. In October 2000 an undercover TV reporter strolled around Germany's parliament building visiting 28 men's toilets and wiping down their surfaces with paper tissues. The tissues were stuffed into airtight tubes and analysed by the Nuremberg-based forensic analyst

Professor Fritz Sorgel. He found that 22 out of the 28 carried traces of cocaine.

Sorgel stressed that his findings might have been distorted by cleaners spreading the drug around on their cloths. Others were less restrained. 'The Parliament of Addicts', declared the tabloid paper *BZ*. Hubert Huppe, the Christian Social Union's narcotics spokesman, pointed out that 'it would be unnatural if parliamentarians were the only group to have nothing to do with drugs'.

THE BUSINESS

One explanation of the tacit acceptance of cocaine among Germany's middle classes is that employers may not necessarily see it as a Bad Thing. At the height of the Bundestag business a leading social scientist, Gunter Amendt, pointed out that whereas marijuana and alcohol were 'employer unfriendly', the big C actually makes staff graft harder. There's nothing new about this idea – for centuries South American plantation owners even paid their workforce with it – but in a nation with Germany's enhanced work ethic you can see how it might appeal.

HARD TO HANDLE?

This is the abiding mystery of cocaine culture. How come some take it without a problem while others watch their personal lives and careers mercilessly shredded? One of the most brilliant economists on Wall Street, Lawrence

Kudlow, was earning $1 million (£700,000) a year when he started snorting as a 25-year-old in 1984. As an adviser to the Reagan administration he was courted and cosseted by the markets to the point that he felt 'indestructible'. Then he began missing client appointments and got himself fired from the investment bank Bear Stearns. The cocaine vice gripped ever stronger; debts mounted; his wife threatened divorce.

In 1995, Kudlow went into five months of rehab. He kicked his addiction, became a devout Christian and, in 2000, regained the giddy heights of Wall Street as chief economist to ING Barings. 'Handling large sums of money can sometimes mislead people into thinking that they are powerful,' he said in one interview in November 2000. 'They are not. I have never blamed Wall Street. It's an attitude, not the pressure. People believe they can turn it on and turn it off and, sooner or later, they realise that they can't.'

Manhattan-based addiction therapist Dr Arnold Washton, founder of America's first cocaine hotline in 1982, sees this all the time. Around a third of his clients work on Wall Street and they tell him they use the drug to feel 'energetic, powerful, sexy and on top of the world'. Washton has little doubt that cocaine is re-emerging as the drug of choice for senior executives. 'It was almost treated as passé for a while,' he told the London *Guardian* (29 November 2000). 'There's a new crop of young, ambitious professionals who find this drug suitable. It fits right in with the tenor of the times.'

It is exactly this attitude that so angers some senior politicians and police officers. On 4 January 1999, Britain's so-called 'drugs tsar', Keith Hellawell, waded into City of London cocaine users. Just because wealth allowed them to buy the drug without thieving, he told BBC Radio 4's *Today* programme, it didn't mean they were innocent of damaging society. 'I wish they'd stop it,' he said. 'There's this arrogance – I call it an intellectual arrogance. If they are dealing with my pension fund on the dealing floors they could be causing me damage. It isn't a joke, it's deadly serious.'

SPORTING SNORTERS

This is another strange facet of the cocaine debate. Sometimes it's funny, sometimes it's not. When the England international footballer Robbie Fowler celebrated a goal at his former club Liverpool FC by kneeling down and running his nose along the white line of the penalty area, everybody under 40 in the crowd had a good laugh. This generation was familiar with cocaine; they knew Fowler was comparing the 'high' of scoring with the 'high' of coke.

Yet for those world-famous sportsmen and women caught using the drug the consequences are stark. When Germany appointed Christoph Daum as trainer of its national football team in 2000 there were widespread rumours that his trademark 'boggle-eyed' expression and legendary short temper were the result of cocaine use. Daum agreed to have a hair sample analysed to prove his innocence. It was the worst result of his career. The test showed he'd consumed large quantities of the drug and the coaching offer was hurriedly withdrawn.

Drug testing has now become so prevalent in sport that for professional players and athletes a line or two of cocaine is no longer worth the risk. American footballer Dexter Manley failed one test while starring for the Washington Redskins in 1989 and then another two years later as a Tampa Bay Buccaneers player. He retired from football but not from cocaine and eventually served 15 months of a four-year drugs sentence.

FREE-FLOWING TRAFFIC

Cocaine consumers may come from all walks of life but the cocaine business has only one spiritual home. It's true that Peru is probably the largest coca leaf grower, that Bolivia harvests a decent crop, that Mexican drug cartels have grabbed a big slice of the US smuggling trade, and that the Caribbean is a key worldwide transiting centre. There are growers and traffickers in Brazil, Venezuela, Argentina, Ecuador, Uruguay and Paraguay, but you could take down every last one and barely register a blip on world supplies. There is only one undisputed king of the cocaine ring. Ask any law-enforcement agency and they'll tell you: 80 per cent of the world's cocaine moves through Colombia.

According to the UN special conference on the global drug problem (New York, 1998) there has been a big reduction in area devoted to the coca bush worldwide. In 1990 this stood at 288,000ha (710,000 acres); by 1998 it was down to 179,000ha (440,000 acres). Yet the production of coca in tonnes/tons has seen a more gradual decline – from 363,981 tonnes/tons in 1990 to around 300,000 in 1998. A combination of improving crop yields (horticultural science doesn't care who it helps) and the spread of new, unidentified plantations probably explains the discrepancy.

Despite a 40 per cent reduction in its coca crop, Peru is theoretically the biggest grower (118,000 tonnes/tons in 1997) followed by Bolivia (93,000 tonnes/tons) and Colombia (91,000 tonnes/tons). By the time this book is published this league table may well have changed, as Colombian guerrillas use coca growing to fund their continuing civil war against the government. What these statistics don't reveal is the proportion of South American coca bought up by Colombians. Put it this way, they don't miss much.

Assuming a conversion rate in which 1,000 tonnes/tons of coca leaf equals 9 tonnes/tons of cocaine, the UN reckons that the total world harvest was upwards of 800 tonnes/tons in 1997. Government seizures accounted for perhaps 300 tonnes/tons, leaving 500–700 tonnes/tons to be smuggled, shuffled, smoked and snorted around the globe. This is almost certainly a massive underestimate, but then that's the United Nations for you.

The UN's *Global Illicit Drug Trends* report for 2001 has cast a little more light on things. It analysed the amount of cocaine actually seized by government forces in 1999. This predictably showed the world's biggest market – America – way out in front with 132,318kg (291,000lbs). Next came Colombia with 63,945kg (140,000lbs) and way behind in third place Mexico with 34,623kg (76,000lbs).

The rest are also-rans. There's Spain (18,111kg/40,000lbs) Venezuela, Peru, The Netherlands, Ecuador and Guatemala (all in the 10,000–12,500kg/22,000–27,500lbs range) and Bolivia and Brazil (each 7,700kg/17,000lbs). The whole of western Europe accounted for 43,707kg (96,000lbs), while in the Caribbean seizures amounted to 12,133kg (26,700lbs).

The report confirmed what everyone already knew: that the main trafficking routes shoot out from the major South and Central American producers and head straight up Uncle Sam's monster pair of nostrils in the north. Cocaine shipments come via road across the US/Mexican border, in 'go-fast' boats up America's Pacific coast and in sea ferries, pleasure boats or commercial planes via the Bahamas, Haiti, Puerto Rico, the Dominican Republic and various other Caribbean islands.

Jamaica is the main air bridge for Colombian cartels accessing Europe and the Middle East. Since the late 1990s these markets have been particularly good at filling traffickers' boots with cash, at only slightly enhanced levels of risk. Whereas a kilo (2¼lbs) of pure cocaine may sell for $20,000 (£14,000) wholesale in Miami, in London it can be worth three times as much. Elsewhere there is some traditional, international trade: Brazil to Angola, Ecuador to Hong Kong or Japan and Argentina to South Africa and Australia. As for smuggling methods, these range from the ingenious to the downright yucky (see below).

WHAT'S ON THE MOVE?

At this point we need to be clear about the type of cocaine being smuggled. If it's a bulk shipment it may be coca paste – *pasta basica* – the same, smokable stuff that so excited those early American traffickers back in the 1970s and later sparked the crack epidemic. If it has already been fully processed it'll be pure(ish) cocaine hydrochloride in ready-to-cut powder form.

Paste is favoured by the big cocaine cartels because it's convenient in size and weight, and dead simple to produce in jungle kitchens from raw coca. The recipe varies from country to country, but essentially you harvest your coca leaves, dry them, chop them up, sprinkle them with cement and soak them in petrol for a day. This leaches out the cocaine alkaloid. You then siphon off the petrol and put the mashed leaves through a press to extract the remaining liquid.

Add a bucket of water containing some drops of car battery acid (one bucket per 30kg/65lbs of leaf), stir and allow to rest. Because the alkaloid is more soluble in acid than in petrol it moves into the acid solution. Chuck in some caustic soda, filter the solidifying murky mess through a cloth, strain and allow to dry into a yellowy-white powder. Here's your paste, somewhere between 40 and 60 per cent pure. If anyone ever tells you that cocaine is a 'natural' drug, ask them about the cement, petrol, battery acid and caustic soda.

In fairness, there are two further steps before the cocaine is ready for market. It has to be dissolved in solvents, allowed to solidify and then washed in another, very pure, solvent to produce 90 per cent pure cocaine hydrochloride. This is usually done by the cartel buyers, who process the paste in their own remote laboratories. It's at this point that the traffickers, and the money movers, queue up to make their millions.

WHO ARE THE MOVERS?

In September 2001 the US Office of Domestic Intelligence (ODI) published a report highlighting recent trends in the Central American cocaine markets. This showed that while Colombia remains the major player, drug cartels there have contracted-out much of their cross-border smuggling business to the Mexicans. Until 1989 Colombians usually paid Mexican traffickers to drive or fly cocaine across the US border (65 per cent of American cocaine enters this way) but had associates in place the other side to take delivery. This ensured that Colombian cartels retained control of wholesale distribution. However, a massive 21 tonne/ton seizure in 1989 led to a new underworld deal.

'By the mid-1990s, Mexico-based transportation groups were receiving up to half the cocaine shipment they smuggled for the Colombia-based groups in exchange for their services,' says the ODI. 'Both sides realised that this strategy eliminated the vulnerabilities and complex logistics associated with large cash transactions. The Colombia-based groups also realised that relinquishing part of each cocaine shipment to their associates operating from Mexico ceded a share of the wholesale cocaine market in the United States.'

According to the ODI there then followed a good old-fashioned carve-up of territory. The Colombians retained control of their lucrative north-east markets and eastern seaboard cities such as Boston, Miami, Newark, New York and Philadelphia. The Mexicans got the west and mid-west, specifically cities such as Chicago, Dallas, Denver, Houston, Los Angeles, Phoenix, San Diego, San Francisco and Seattle. Both sides made alliances with Dominican underworld groups (traditionally responsible for street-level distribution), particularly in New York City.

It's not that Colombian drug lords didn't have the stomach for a turf war. It's just that they didn't see the point. When you make $10 million (£7 million) a day, why worry if it drops to $5 million (£3.5 million), especially if the risks are spread. More to the point, there was that horrible word 'extradition', which had never really been part of the Colombian vocabulary. From 17 December 1997, however, any Colombian mafia boss drug running overtly to the USA knew it was likely to lead to an appointment with an American judge. And a long, long time to think about what went wrong.

When a Colombian or Mexican drug lord dies accidentally or through natural causes no one ever believes it. People just assume the man concerned has faked his own death in order to acquire a clean new identity. This is why good plastic surgeons are never idle in Central America. However, treating mafia bosses is not without the occasional setback, chief among which is the patient dying on the operating table. Drug families are never very understanding about that sort of thing.

So when Amado Carrillo Fuentes – the single most powerful cocaine baron in the Americas during the mid-1990s – apparently died while undergoing liposuction and cosmetic surgery at Mexico City's Santa Monica hospital, the country's response was to look for a set-up. The patient had checked in under the name of Antonio Flores Montes and the bruised and surgically scarred corpse was simply assumed to be some convenient victim hauled in as Carrillo's dead body double. This was not the view of the chief surgeon, who promptly fled the country. Neither was it the opinion of the DEA, FBI or the Mexican police – all of whom declared fingerprint and DNA analysis as conclusive proof that the cadaver was Carrillo. Champagne corks must have popped in Washington DC that night.

The trouble is that killing cartel leaders – even big fish like Carrillo – makes not a jot of difference to cocaine street sales. The DEA admits as much in its website analysis of leading Colombian and Mexican traffickers. 'Until recently, the Colombian trafficking organizations, collectively known as the Cali mafia, dominated the international cocaine market. Although some elements of the Cali mafia continue to play an important role in the world's wholesale cocaine market, events in recent years – including the capture of the Rodriguez-Orejuela brothers in 1995, the death of Jose Santacruz-Londono in March 1996 and the surrender of Pacho Herrera in September 1996 – have accelerated the decline of the Cali mafia influence.

'Other experienced traffickers, who have been active for years but worked in the shadow of the Cali drug lords, have successfully seized opportunities to increase their share of the drug trade...Independent Colombian traffickers are still responsible for most of the world's cocaine production and wholesale distribution.'

This is the problem for western governments. For every cocaine godfather taken down, six more are clamouring to nab his markets. It's the same with the drug couriers. As police and customs technology gets better, so the smuggling gets sneakier.

DELIVERING THE GOODIES

Here's the scale of the problem facing the United States Customs Service (USCS). According to its own statistics, 60 million people arrive in America on more than 675,000 commercial and private flights each year. Another 370 million come by land and 6 million by sea. Around 116 million vehicles cross the land borders with Canada and Mexico. Upwards of 90,000 merchant and passenger ships enter American ports carrying a combined total of 9 million shipping containers and 400 million tonnes/tons of cargo. In addition, 157,000 smaller vessels visit the harbours of coastal towns. Would you know the enemy? Exactly.

A quick tally reveals 436 million people arriving every year. The vast majority are good, decent law-abiding citizens, but the task of picking out the bad guys falls to just 7,500 USCS officers at 301 ports of entry. The odds are not great but the USCS, the US Coast Guard, the Navy, DEA, FBI and CIA undoubtedly do disrupt drug smuggling effectively. There are 26 customs jets on interdiction deployment with smuggler 'host countries'. Customs P3 aircraft mount continuous surveillance over the Andean mountains to identify potential drug planes, and over the eastern Pacific to spot suspicious inbound ships. Fast Coast Guard cutters patrol the Caribbean and Pacific trafficking corridors.

Of the 86,700kg (190,000lbs) of cocaine seized in the USA during the fiscal year 2001, 40,000kg (88,000lbs) was being taken across the US/Mexican border. It's easy to see why. The border is mostly desert, unpopulated, unpatrolled, unfenced, and stretches for 3,200km (2,000 miles). The US government does its best with radar balloons and the odd surveillance aircraft but, frankly, you could march a couple of battalions across before anyone noticed. Most smugglers still use the tarmac roads, but as there aren't very many of these congestion causes a different set of problems. At the entry point of San Ysidro, south of San Diego, 20,000 pedestrians and 96,000 car passengers travel across the world's busiest land border post every day.

Among the hi-tech gadgets used by customs officers to monitor this mass of humanity is something called a 'density-buster': a kind of ultrasound scanner that can tell, for instance, whether your tyres contain more than just air. Digital cameras photograph 40,000 car registration plates a day, simultaneously checking them against national databases of suspect cars. On the USA side, metal tyre shredders can be raised from the road to stop drivers crashing through inspection booths. But the best way of rooting out cocaine stashes is to use the most unbelievably sensitive drug-odour detectors known to man: dogs.

In March 2001 one attempt to keep sniffer mutts at bay involved packing 1,000kg (2,200lbs) of cocaine into a trailer carrying pallets of onions. It was stopped by police in rural Hidalgo County on the Texas/Mexico border and escorted to the Pharr port of entry for examination. The powerful smell of the onions didn't seem to worry sniffer dog Scar, who immediately alerted them to the presence of drugs.

Customs officers tell stories of wised-up traffickers vacuum-sealing cocaine, smearing the package in grease, sealing it again and sinking it into a car petrol tank. Doesn't work. Dogs such as German shepherds – one of several breeds used by the USCS – have 220 million sensory cells in their noses, compared to just five million in humans. They can thoroughly check a car in six minutes. Even a cursory search by officers would take 20.

GO CREATE!

Tried and trusted smuggling methods include false compartments in suitcases and aerosol spray cans, false soles in shoes, swallowing 'bullets' (small amounts of coke wrapped in plastic or condoms and swallowed), solutions of cocaine in wine or brandy bottles, baby powder containers – the list goes on. But as detection techniques are improving, smugglers are having to think more creatively. On 26 February 2001, customs special agents raided a bungalow in Nogales, Arizona, where they found a 7.5m- (25ft-) long hand-dug tunnel linked to the city's sewer system. Given that 198 cocaine bricks were found in the front room, and that Mexico lay three-quarters of a mile to the south, it's clear what was happening.

THE HIGH SEAS

American successes on land are more than matched by results at sea. In 2000 and 2001 there was a string of record-breaking marine seizures involving cocaine. Using boats is a huge gamble for traffickers because it's obviously impossible to spread risk. You can send 100 drug mules through an airport and if two-thirds make it the losses are manageable. But if your boat gets busted, it's painful – even for a cartel boss.

Yet moving cocaine by sea seems as popular as ever, at least if seizure figures announced by the White House Office of National Drug Control Policy (ONDCP) are any guide. In October 2001 its acting director, Edward Jurith, revealed that 62,800kg (138,334lbs) of the drug was recovered by US Coast Guard vessels over the previous 12 months: almost 2,700kg (6,000lbs) more than the previous record (set the previous year). This can mean one of three things:

- the Coast Guard is getting better or luckier;
- there's more cocaine on the ocean;
- both of the above.

Jurith had no doubt that pooling international resources was the key. He told a Washington DC press conference (5 October 2001) that, 'This increase in seizures takes place at the same time that other data tell us US consumers are using an ever-smaller proportion of the world's cocaine. Seizing more from a smaller universe of drugs is exactly what supply reduction aims to do. Much of the success is due to international cooperation, information-sharing and targeted operations. Foreign governments are also doing better – and for many of the same reasons.'

Of the 2001 successes, by far the greatest was the boarding of the Belize-flagged fishing boat *Svesda Maru* on 3 May 2001. This 45m (150ft) vessel was first sighted on

28 April by one of US Customs' P3 aircraft. Its position in the eastern Pacific was reported the following day by a Coast Guard C-130 patrol plane, and a decision was made to despatch a US Navy guided missile frigate carrying specialist search teams. After five days they discovered a large, unexplained area beneath the fish holds: at least it was unexplained until they found a 12,000kg (26,400lbs) stash of cocaine. This single seizure was the biggest in maritime history, equivalent to one-sixteenth of the entire cocaine haul confiscated on mainland America that year.

It wasn't just American agencies that broke seizure records in 2001. On 27 July Federal police recovered Australia's largest single cocaine consignment soon after it was offloaded from a 30m (100ft) fishing boat in Dulverton Bay, a remote stretch of the western Australian coast some 650km (400 miles) north of Perth. Around 1,000kg (2,200lbs) of cocaine were buried on a lonely beach and soon afterwards the boat sank in what police euphemistically called 'inexplicable circumstances'. Five people were arrested.

In March 2002 it was the British government's turn to celebrate. After a joint surveillance operation and raid by Her Majesty's Customs and Excise and the National Crime Squad (NCS), five marine traffickers were jailed for a total of 99 years. They had been caught red-handed offloading 400kg (880lbs) of cocaine to a safe house on the Isle of Wight, off southern England. This, too, was a record cocaine seizure.

CRACKDOWN

Three months after the attacks on the World Trade Center and the Pentagon, US Customs Commissioner Robert Bonner pointed out that America's war on terrorism was also bad news for traffickers. 'Contrary to what some might believe, the counter-terrorism and counter-narcotics missions are not mutually exclusive,' he said. 'One does not necessarily come at the expense of the other. Everyone...knows that there is a nexus between drug trafficking and terrorism. Everyone in Colombia knows this' (speech to the 2001 National High Intensity Drug Trafficking Areas (HIDTA) conference, Washington DC, 6 December 2001).

The tightening of America's domestic security briefly took its toll on land-based Mexican and Colombian cocaine operations. Cross-border runs were delayed as the underworld waited for things to calm down. 'In the end they got fed up waiting and carried on regardless,' USCS officer Dean Boyd told me. 'We saw cocaine seizures pick up in the fall of 2001 and early 2002. This was partly because we were deploying more people to counter terrorism along our borders. [The events of] 11 September did disrupt road trafficking – but not for long. We soon saw cocaine smugglers back down their usual routes. They knew, and we knew, that they had buyers waiting.'

For the air mules it was a different story. Before 11 September, 50 per cent of all drugs found on passengers arriving in the USA came from flights originating in Jamaica. Given that the island generates less than 3 per cent of US air traffic, this is some achievement. However, after the terrorist attacks, getting drugs through American airports became a nightmare. There was a sense that US air authorities had been too complacent in the past and they sure as hell weren't about to make the same mistake again. In Jamaica supplies built up. European markets, with their traditional high prices and expanding street dealerships, suddenly seemed more attractive than ever.

Superintendent Gladstone Wright of the Jamaican Constabulary Narcotics Division put it like this: 'In terms of what is happening in Britain, the trade has escalated sharply since 11 September. The couriers who would normally be travelling to America are unable to get their drugs through because security at the borders has become so tight. Cocaine is stockpiling in Jamaica and that is no good for the dealers. There is no viable market for the drug here. So it is all being diverted to Britain.

'Becoming a drug mule is the most readily available form of employment in this country at the moment. It is a job that you do not need to be interviewed for, or have any kind of qualifications, but you can earn more money than most Jamaicans see in a lifetime. The economy here is very bad at the moment and unemployment among women is running at 22 per cent. These people are easy prey for the dealers' (London *Observer*, 6 January 2002).

The Netherlands' Schiphol Airport has become another key destination for British and European distribution. Police estimate that between 20,000 and 25,000 mules pass through the terminal each year, most of them Dutch citizens flying on return tickets from the former Caribbean colonies of the Antilles and Surinam. Government figures for 2001 show that 1,200 air passengers were convicted of cocaine trafficking, a 60 per cent increase on the previous year. Those who escaped arrest and made their delivery would have been paid around £2,000 ($2,900) plus expenses.

The situation at Schiphol got so bad after 11 September that, in January 2002, senior customs officers wrote a letter to the Amsterdam daily newspaper *Het Parool* complaining that they'd been ordered to stop arresting cocaine traffickers. The reason? Dutch jails were too full to take any more felons. This was despite the fact that during random checks on one flight from the Caribbean, no fewer than 40 smugglers had been caught. 'At a time when our society is being flooded with drugs,' the customs team wrote, 'we are being forced on the express orders of our superiors to stick our heads in the sand.'

They recounted one ludicrous case in which a woman found with 14kg (30lb) of coke in her luggage was released because no cell was available for her. Her £460,000 ($666,000) consignment was confiscated but she demanded – and got – a police receipt to prove to her drugs masters that she hadn't sold off the goodies herself.

HARD TO SWALLOW?

Of all the mules, the 'body packers' adopt the most ignominious technique. They prepare for their ordeal by swallowing whole grapes. Shortly before their flight they switch to compressed cocaine encased in the severed finger pieces of latex rubber gloves. These are sealed into pellets by a special machine and coated with honey to help prevent gagging. The sealing part of the process isn't quite perfect. This is probably why at least ten mules died of cocaine poisoning during 2001 while waiting to board flights at Kingston Airport.

Once the pellets are swallowed (payment is per pellet and swallowers are believed to manage anywhere between 30 and 120 in a single sitting) the mule will take a large dose of anti-diarrhoea tablets to induce constipation. After the flight there's then a six-day wait for nature to take its course.

How did it come to this? How did supposedly civilized societies reduce their citizens to swallowing rubber gloves filled with chemically laden drugs to be crapped out and handed to others to mix with yet more chemicals so that different people would pay big bucks to snort or smoke them and feel cool? I mean, you couldn't make it up. All this nonsense over one ordinary little plant.

Time for a history lesson.

HISTORY

FOOD OF THE GODS

Who knows how it happened: how the very first South American became the very first coke-head? It would have been several thousand, maybe tens of thousands of years ago, that this 'First User' would have ripped off a bunch of coca leaves and taken a tentative chew to check out the taste.

Suppose this Indian – let's call them Charlie for obvious and convenient reasons – tried to improve the flavour and texture by adding a touch of alkali. This could have been burned roots, powdered lime, seashells or anything else in the native diet with a high pH. Alkalis like these leach out the rush-giving alkaloids from coca.

There's no doubt that over the next few hours this primitive equivalent of chewing gum would have made Charlie feel cool about, say, hunting guanaco for that day's dinner. It wouldn't have matched the coked-up buzz enjoyed by today's users as most coca leaves contain less than 1 per cent cocaine. To get a 21st-century-style high Charlie would have had to dry the leaves, pound them up and consume 50g-worth (1¾oz) in one mega-snort.

Even so, the leaves would have produced a gradual onset of euphoria and well-being, a marked lack of hunger and fatigue, and heightened mental alertness. Within a few generations coca would have progressed in Indian culture from unremarkable shrub to food of the gods.

This version of events is admittedly light on fact. But, in essence, it is true. South American Indians were the first people to use coca simply because it didn't grow anywhere else. It has become a defining part of their culture, helps them work longer and harder, performs wonders as an anaesthetic (the Inca seemed very keen on it for brain surgery), treats snow blindness, stomach upsets, headaches and altitude sickness, and even, so it turns out, provides some useful nutrition.

COCA ROOTS

Coca is a member of the genus *Erythroxylum*, of which there are around 250 species, mostly native to South America and all heavily reliant on wet, frost-free, warm, humid growing conditions. It grows faster at sea level but its cocaine yield increases at altitude and most commercial plantations are found at heights between 450 and 1,800m (1,500 and 6,000ft). As a result, the continent's prime cocaine belt runs from Colombia in the north, down the eastern foothills of the Andes to southern Bolivia and the eastern edge of the Amazon basin. Many, though not all, species contain cocaine although only a few contain enough to make cultivation worth the candle. Of these few, four in particular have cornered the market.

- **_Erythroxylum_ variety _cocacoca_.** Usually known as Bolivian coca, this was for many years the biggest source of illegal cocaine. It still plays a major role in Bolivia's agricultural economy and, according to the United Nations Drug Control Programme, the country's total annual harvest is currently around 93,000 tonnes/tons.
- **_Erythroxylum novogranatense_.** This one is native to Colombia – a region known as Nueva Granada (New Granada) to Spanish colonists – hence the plant's name. This was the first coca leaf seen by white Europeans and its cocaine was later exported all over the world as a legal, medical anaesthetic. For years it never much featured in international trafficking; at least not until the big Colombian cartels decided during the 1980s that they could expand profit margins by growing their own instead of importing from Bolivia and Peru. It was a canny move, given that novogranatense now services 85 per cent of the world's illegal cocaine market.
- **_Erythroxylum novogranatense_ variety _truxillense_.** Better known as Trujillo, this flourishes in the dry, coastal desert strip around the Peruvian city of the same name. Because of the climate, Trujillo can only grow in well-irrigated plantations but its flavoursome leaves and high cocaine content made it well worth the effort for Inca

tribes who knew it as 'Royal Coca'. Mother Nature gets particularly motherly where Trujillo is concerned because its cocaine content is a total nightmare to extract commercially. For this reason it has never been much use to traffickers, although it is the leaf of choice for the manufacturers of Coca-Cola. In case you were wondering, coca leaves are still used to give Coca-Cola its flavour – but only after the cocaine has been removed. So when right-wing politicians and middle-aged golfers finger-wag you at drinks parties and demand to know why the world coca crop can't just be blitzed by the CIA, you can tell them the truth. It's to keep the world's greatest soft drink up there as market leader. Besides, Bacardi doesn't taste as good on its own.

- *Erythroxylum coca* **variety** *ipadu.* Another coca variety which, until the last two decades, rarely interested traffickers because of its fairly low cocaine count. It is native to the Amazon basin and has been chewed by Indians there for aeons. The war on drugs and drug plantations by western governments has increasingly forced growers to look to *ipadu* and the Amazon as a safer, discreet source.

A DIRECT LINE TO THE PAST
There are two sources for the history of coca: archaeological (still somewhat patchy) – and written, which begins when Francisco Pizarro and his conquistadors

conquered the Inca in 1532. For many years the prehistoric archaeology of South America was dominated by a view that human occupation began well after 18000 BC, when an Ice Age Arctic land bridge allowed Asian migrants to colonize what are now Alaska and Canada. The theory was supported by the carbon dating of tools and weapons of the Stone Age Clovis people, whose cultures were widespread further south, to around 10000 BC.

Then, in 1977, discoveries at Monte Verde, southern Chile, by the American archaeologist Tom Dillehay turned all this on its head. Radiocarbon tests showed that much of the material he unearthed was laid down in 11000 BC, opening the possibility that hunter-gatherer people were living in the southern Andes as early as 31000 BC.

The Monte Verde tribe's religion was apparently important enough for labour to be assigned to the construction of a ritual temple. It had gravel footings, wooden stakes strengthening its walls and a central platform. Here Dillehay's team found remnants of medicinal plants (though not coca): an indication that the temple was used for healing ceremonies as well as perhaps ancestor worship.

The word coca is thought by many anthropologists to derive from khoka, which literally meant 'the plant' in the tongue of the pre-Incan Tiwanaku people. Centred on Lake Titicaca, this culture developed a highly efficient agricultural system in which raised beds and shoreline canals lengthened the growing season. For these farmers to christen coca *the* plant – as opposed to any old plant – gives some idea of their regard for it. Tiwanaku dates from at least the 3rd century AD, declining around AD 1000, and its legacy is the Quechuan language spoken by ten million people from Ecuador to Argentina.

By the time the Inca arrived on the scene, coca production had really taken off. The Inca were a remarkable people. They transformed themselves from a 12th-century minor tribe confined to a 30km (20 mile) radius of Cuzco, in Peru's Cordillera region, to become masters of an empire stretching for some 3,500km (2,175 miles) north to south and 800km (500 miles) east to west. And they achieved all this in under 100 years.

It was the eighth Inca (ie emperor) Viracocha who began seizing new territory in 1437. But it was his son Pachacuti, grandson Topa and great-grandson Huayna Capac who really caught the empire-building bug. By the time Huayna died in 1525 Inca influence stretched from what is now southern Colombia, through Ecuador and Peru and on to Bolivia, northern Argentina and Chile: a total population of anything up to 16 million.

Their power was rooted in natural aggression and superb organization. The fact that people worshipped the emperor as a living god certainly helped – no wishy-washy democracy here. Good communications across the empire were crucial: the four administrative areas were linked by a 24,000km (15,000 mile) network of stone roads, tunnels and vine suspension bridges. These were reserved for teams of state-appointed messengers capable of covering 400km (250 miles) per day. Food production was organized on rigid 'communist' lines, with government experts choosing crops, supervising irrigation, terracing and fertilization, and taking a share of the harvest to store in times of need. A healthy percentage of this would have been coca. In fact, coca was key to the whole shebang. It was the centre of religious life.

Inca religion regarded the leaf as divine and magical. Priests used it for offerings, chewed it during rituals (and in the presence of the emperor), burnt it to ensure its glorious aroma pleased the gods, scattered its ashes to keep the fertility goddess Pachamama happy and placed it with the dead to stop spirits returning to the land of the living.

Predicting the future was part of a high priest's job and if there was one thing Inca folk liked in a priest it was divination. Oracles were consulted over everything from sickness to criminal investigations and, most importantly, the timing of sacrifices. Conclusions could be drawn from simple rituals – watching the path of a spider in an upturned bowl – to messier ones such as inspecting the marks on sacrificed llama lungs. Inevitably, coca was right up there as a divination aid. Leaves would be flung into the air or thrown on to liquid and 'read' according to how they landed.

Young men from high-ranking families would sometimes undergo a fearsome initiation into manhood, which could involve flogging, racing and sparring. More commonly this rite of passage took the form of a simple race in which the final straight was lined by young women making suggestive quips and offering coca or *chicha* (weak beer). Finishers, or survivors, were rewarded with a sling and a coca pouch marking their emergence into manhood. Even today, one Colombian tribe still practises an initiation ritual in which candidates 'marry' the coca leaf.

Perhaps because of its special place in Inca society, some historians have argued that coca was restricted to an elite. There's no doubt that it was, literally, close to the heart of the Inca (emperor) himself, because the only object he ever carried was the coca pouch around his neck. Two emperors even named their wives after the leaf, using the sacred title *Mama Coca*. Only two other crops were credited with the *Mama* prefix: maize and cinchona.

Other important state officials would have been allocated coca rations as a perk or necessity of the job: priests, doctors, magicians, warriors, leaders of defeated tribes, memorizers of state records (the Inca never bothered with writing) and those fleet-footed messengers. This is not to say that ordinary people were banned from using it. Given that coca had been around for millennia before the Inca, this would have been a hopeless task. Besides, why ban it? Judging by the huge plantations in the Huánuco Valley and at Yungas in Bolivia, there was no shortage. Far more sensible to concentrate on controlling production and distribution, much in the style of the Chilean government before General Pinochet.

OLD-STYLE CONSUMPTION

Traditional methods of consuming coca have continued unchanged since Charlie and co first got high. A user grabs a few leaves from his personal coca pouch or *chuspa*, wedges them between his teeth and cheek and starts working in a bit of saliva. Then he takes out his *iscupuru*, a gourd containing a concentrated, highly caustic alkaline like powdered shells or roots, and removes a smidgen with a stick.

This powder, known as *llipta* to the Indians, is then carefully pushed into the middle of the coca wad, raising pH levels in the mouth and increasing the speed with which cocaine alkaloids are leached out of the leaf wad. There's a bit of a knack to it. You're not so much chewing as occasionally manipulating the wad with your tongue to keep it moist and exposed to saliva. And one slip with your *llipta* and you've got an internal mouth burn that makes the world's hottest madras feel like cold yoghurt. To guard against this, Indian mothers introducing their children to coca will often 'mix' the *llipta* themselves before transferring it to the child's mouth.

The most obvious effect is that your saliva turns bright green. However, you tend not to worry about this because your mouth is already tingling pleasantly and your throat feels like it's having an out-of-body experience. You have no interest in food and you feel ready to hit the road running. It is by all accounts a far less intense rush than you'd get snorting a line in your neighbourhood club toilets, but because the coca is releasing alkaloids gradually this 'slow rush' persists for much longer.

There is, incidentally, a continuing medical debate about whether the South American chewer, or *coqueros*, are unreconstructed coke addicts or simply 'social' chewers – much in the way western medics will argue the toss about social drinking and alcoholism. Some say your typical *coqueros* has a daily intake of around 15mg, that's about the amount of caffeine in a strong cup of coffee. Others reckon it's closer to half a gram of pure cocaine, which in western street terms is a hefty habit. There are all sorts of sophistry in this kind of debate, but one thing is certain. To a *coqueros*, coca is as much a part of life as a cold beer is to a steel worker. Two different cultures. Two different drugs. Same outrage if anyone suggests a ban.

COCA AND THE CONQUISTADORS
One of the great things about the Spanish (and if you were an Inca Indian there weren't many) is that their explorers in the Americas kept detailed diaries. These reveal fascinating early impressions of coca, including the one reprinted below, which was noted down during the fourth voyage of Christopher Columbus, who sailed from Cadiz in May 1502.

The lieutenant went into the country with 40 men, a boat following with 40 more. The next day they came to the river Urisa, seven leagues west from Belem. The cacique [tribe leader] came a league out of the town to meet him with some 20 men and presented him with such things as they feed on and some gold plates were exchanged here. This cacique and his chief man never ceased putting dry herb into their mouths, which they chewed, and sometimes they took a sort of powder, which they carried along with that herb, which singular custom astonished our people very much.

The Italian navigator Amerigo Vespucci was also baffled by coca. He came across it when he landed on the island of Santa Margarita, off Venezuela, in 1499, and was immediately revolted by the way its 'loathsome' people chewed it. In one letter, published five years later, he included the following report.

'They all had their cheeks swollen out with a green herb inside, which they were constantly chewing like beasts so they could scarcely utter speech: and each one had upon his neck two dried gourds, one of which was full of that herb, which they kept in their mouths, and the other full of a white flour, which looked like powdered chalk and from time to time with a small stick, which they kept moistening in their mouths, they dipped it into the flour and then put it into their mouths in both cheeks... This they did very frequently. And, marvelling at such a thing, we were unable to comprehend their secret.'

Others were more positive. In 1609 Garcilaso de la Vega's classic account of the history and conquest of the Inca, *Royal Commentaries of Peru*, carried a priest's account of coca medicine. 'Our doctors use it in powdered form to reduce the swelling of wounds, to strengthen broken bones, to expel cold from the body or prevent it entering, and to cure rotten wounds or sores that are full of maggots. And if it does so much for outward ailments, will not its singular virtue have even greater effect in the entrails of those who eat it?'

THE COCA CONQUERORS

Vespucci was by no means the only European interested in this strange new world. Spanish adventurers were on the hunt for a fast buck – namely gold and silver – and they had the comfort of knowing that God was on their side. They knew this because the pope had given them the Inca empire back in 1493, in a way that only popes can. They therefore wasted no time in claiming vast territories for Spain and sending home horror stories of the unChristian cannibals and barbarians who passed for human beings. This in turn provided a sensible reason to kill as many as possible, a task the Spanish embraced with enthusiasm. Yet they were outnumbered by hundreds of thousands of Inca warriors. How did it happen? How could it happen?

In fact, the Inca empire was on borrowed time from the moment it first encountered white Europeans. The Indians had no natural immunity to the diseases imported by sailors – plague, smallpox and measles all probably figured – and, by 1527, something like 200,000 Inca had died. The Spanish were firmly in control: the only problem for them was to find something worth controlling. The rivers of gold they had expected to find were just not flowing and the only commodity the Indians really seemed to rate was this strange plant called coca.

CHEWING OVER THE POSSIBILITIES

Coca did nothing for the Spanish. Chewing was a revolting habit and you couldn't export the stuff – even if a European market existed – because it rotted so easily. That said, they were never ones to pass up a business opportunity and it seemed there was very little the Indians wouldn't do for coca. Gradually the settlers saw there was good money in plantations. Production went through the roof and the chewing habit spread even further than it had under the Inca.

Meanwhile, some Europeans began following up old legends about mountains that were made of silver. All these leads pointed to one place, Potosí, in what is now southern Bolivia, a mining area abandoned by the Inca after volcanic rumblings convinced them that the gods were angry. The Spanish had no such fears and when silver was rediscovered there in 1546 it was boom time. Inside a year a new city had been founded and 7,000 Indians were soon digging away, removing 70 tonnes/tons a year. Contemporary records suggest that in 1549 the Spanish crown's one-fifth share was something around 40,000 pesos per week. Potosí expanded exponentially until, by 1611, it had a population of 150,000. Yet all the time the mines got deeper and the Indians worked harder. They needed something that would sustain them. Guess what they chose...?

In 1548 the miners of Potosí chewed their way through more than 1 million kg (almost 1,000 tonnes/tons) of coca. Most wanted to be paid in coca (hard currencies such as the peso were a mystery to them) and so plantations pushed up production to meet demand. Everyone was getting rich, especially the mine owners. They sold silver ore to the smelters and overpriced coca to their workers.

HOLIER THAN THOU?

While Spain counted her cash, the Roman Catholic Church got increasingly stuffy about the coca business. The First Council of Lima in 1552 heard talk of the plant as the devil's work and a form of idolatry, and demanded it be banned. With a smooth bit of spindoctoring, Philip II's father, Charles I of Spain, absolutely agreed and absolutely refused. The Second Council had another go 15 years later, this time hearing that coca encouraged 'demonic influences' and made women infertile. Again the Crown looked the other way. By the time of the Third Council, Philip II had got the hint and agreed that the Church should take a 10 per cent cut of all coca sales. Suddenly priests were commenting on how useful the leaf was to labourers. And for the next 200 years coca and South America carried on pretty much as usual.

THE BOFFINS TAKE A TRIP

In 1786 coca was classified by the biologist Jean Chevalier de Lamarck as *Erythroxylum coca*. Now scientists knew what it was. They just didn't know how it worked.

Biochemistry was, at this time, little more than pseudo-science. Biologists were beginning to look at the natural chemicals in plants as potential medicines; the hard bit was to isolate them. In 1803 the German apothecary FWA Setürner successfully extracted morphine from opium. Strychnine, quinine, caffeine, nicotine and atropine were discovered over the next 30 years and science began grouping these and other nitrogen-based organic compounds as 'alkaloids'. The problem with coca, as we already know, is that it was a nightmare to export. There was never enough good-quality leaf on which to experiment.

In 1859 the breakthrough came. The celebrated German organic chemist Friedrich Wöhler arranged for a colleague working in Peru to bring back a 13.5kg (30lb) bale of coca. He then handed this to one of his best students, Albert Niemann, who analysed it for his PhD. He washed the leaves in 85 per cent alcohol with a little sulphuric acid, distilled the alcohol to leave a sticky residue, separated this into a resin and shook that repeatedly with bicarbonate of soda. The end result was a palmful of small, rod-shaped crystals. As all the other alkaloids ended in 'ine' Niemann thought it right to follow suit. He named his compound coca-ine.

Niemann died the following year, aged just 26, not realising the magnitude of what he had done. Initially, neither did anyone else in the scientific community, but when word spread about an Italian doctor called Paolo Mantegazza, who enthusiastically published the results of coca experiments on himself, eyebrows were raised. Mantegazza's paper, entitled 'Coca Experiences', told how after a dose of 12g (⅓oz) he began leaping over his desk and felt himself 'capable of jumping on my neighbours' heads'. After 54g (1½oz), chewed over an entire day, he was really buzzing.

'I sneered at all the poor mortals condemned to live in the valley of tears while I, carried on the wings of two leaves of coca, went flying through the spaces of 77,438 worlds, each more splendid than the one before. An hour later I was sufficiently calm to write these words with a steady hand: God is unjust because he made man incapable of sustaining the effects of coca all life long. I would rather live a life of ten years with coca than one of 100,000 (and here I inserted a line of zeros) without it.'

Gradually, doctors began to suspect cocaine had its uses. Another self-experimenter was none other than Sir Robert Christison, 78-year-old president of The British

Medical Association. He told *The British Medical Journal* that during two 24km (15 mile) rambles, attempted with and without coca, he felt a huge energy boost when using the leaf.

'I was surprised to find that all sense of weariness had vanished and that I could proceed not only with ease but with elasticity,' he said. Later, Sir Robert told how, after leading some students to the top of a 1,000m (3,280ft) Scottish mountain, he had chewed a little coca for the return trip.

'I at once felt that all fatigue was gone and I went down the long descent with an ease which felt like that which I used to enjoy in the mountainous rambles in my youth,' he noted. '... The chewing of coca not only removes extreme fatigue, but prevents it. Hunger and thirst are suspended; but eventually appetite and digestion are unaffected. No injury is sustained at the time or subsequently in occasional trials.'

THE FIRST COCAINE USERS

While the boffins were somewhat slow off the mark, big business quickly recognized cocaine's potential. Among the first entrepreneurs to exploit the mass market was a Corsican apothecary called Angelo Mariani, who in 1863 hit on the idea of mixing the drug with wine.

The taste was pleasant enough but the real advantage was that alcohol worked as a solvent, extracting cocaine alkaloids from the leaf. Soon everyone in polite society had heard of Vin Mariani.

COCA UNDER THE MICROSCOPE

While all this was going on, science at last got its act together. A promising young Austrian research student called Sigmund Freud read about cocaine experiments carried out on Bavarian soldiers by a Dr Theodore Aschenbrandt. Aschenbrandt's idea was to look at military applications for the drug and, clearly, an army on wizzo marching powder would be, as early enemies of the Inca discovered, some army.

Freud clearly thought it was a wonderful drug (judging by the free samples he sent out to colleagues and friends) and he found it a great way to alleviate bouts of depression (of which he had many). However, it seems he loved it a little too much. The paper he produced later, 'About Coca', could almost have been written by a coke-head, talking of 'the most gorgeous excitement' shown by animals injected with the drug and referring to 'offerings' rather than 'doses'. It was not exactly scientific language.

IT'S A KNOCKOUT…

Freud would go on to invent psychoanalysis and be generally considered one of the 20th century's most innovative – or barmy – thinkers, depending on your point of view. But the future of cocaine was entwined with the fate of a younger colleague, the medical student Carl Koller, with whom Freud had been cooperating in cocaine experiments. Koller was obsessed with finding better anaesthetics, particularly for eye surgery. Knocking out patients with ether was hopeless (a) because those in frail condition might never recover and (b) because in coming round patients often vomited violently, tearing fragile sutures.

Koller had noticed that when pure cocaine touched his lips it made them feel numb. He'd mentioned this to Freud with little response, but when another colleague casually remarked that the new drug 'numbed the tongue' realisation dawned. Koller dashed to a nearby laboratory and immediately conducted experiments: first on the eyes of a frog and then on his own eyes. He found that after applying a cocaine solution he could touch the cornea with a pinhead and feel nothing. On 15 September 1884 his discovery of the world's first local anaesthetic was placed before an astounded audience at the Heidelberg Ophthalmological Society's annual convention. One of medicine's most challenging problems had been solved by a mere 27-year-old intern.

Sigmund Freud was frustrated by Koller's triumph but he soon had more important things to worry about. That same year he was attempting to provide pain relief for his great friend Dr Ernst von Fleischl-Marxow, who had an excruciating nerve condition. Fleischl-Marxow had resorted to morphine to help him sleep and had become addicted. Freud offered him cocaine as an alternative. Inside 20 days, Freud reported later, all trace of the morphine craving had vanished while 'no cocaine habituation set in; on the contrary, an increasing antipathy to the drug was unmistakably evident'.

Of course, Freud was wrong. The morphine habit had simply been replaced by a cocaine habit, and in April 1885, barely a year after Fleischl-Marxow first tried the new drug, he was in bits and pieces. Freud discovered he was injecting a full gram of cocaine solution every day and suffered from fits and fainting. Worse, the patient experienced a horrendous physical ordeal in which he believed insects were crawling around underneath his skin. He would sit staring at an arm or leg for long periods trying to pinch one out. Fleischl-Marxow was, in fact, suffering hallucinations caused by cocaine toxosis: the dreaded 'coke bugs'.

To his horror, Freud realised that he had produced the world's first cocaine addict. He began warning friends that they should now be extremely careful with the samples he'd sent them. What he did not know was that Fleischl-Marxow had also created a piece of social history by inventing the 'speedball', a dose of cocaine and morphine (or heroin) taken simultaneously.

He found that the stimulant effects of cocaine worked well alongside the 'downer' offered by morphine and that this combination taken intravenously helped get him through the day. When Freud discovered the truth he hoped and believed that his friend would die in six months. In fact Fleischl-Marxow's tortured body held out for six more years. The fundamentally flawed belief that cocaine could be used to treat morphine addicts persisted well into the 20th century.

BIRTH OF A GLOBAL BRAND

For a brief time, cocaine was viewed as a wonder drug, both by qualified doctors and the less-scrupulous quack-potions industry. It was certainly seized upon as a potential cure for morphine and opium use (a particularly serious problem in America where many Civil War veterans had returned to civvy street as junkies). An Atlanta pharmacist called John Pemberton was one of these addicts and in 1880 he decided to copy Mariani's idea of mixing coca with wine, producing his own uninspiringly named French Wine Coca. He marketed it as a general tonic and morphine substitute, and claimed it was regularly knocked back by 20,000 of the world's greatest scientists.

Things were looking good for Pemberton until 1885, when Atlanta's politicians banned all alcoholic drinks. Undeterred he went back to his laboratory and came up with a new concoction, mostly coca leaves and caffeine-rich kola nuts, sold through chemists as a concentrated syrup that buyers diluted with water or soda water. Pemberton needed a snappy trade name and by swapping the 'k' in kola for a 'c' he came up with something called Coca-Cola. Sounds vaguely familiar, doesn't it?.

The drink didn't take off as Pemberton hoped and after six years he flogged the rights to an ex-medical student called Asa Griggs Candler for $2,300 (£1,600). It proved good business for Candler. When he took over, sales stood at 40,000 litres (9,000 gal) of syrup a year. Ten years later, at the turn of the century, he was shifting 1.7 million litres (370,877 gal) and, by the time he died in 1929, his personal fortune had topped $50 million (£34.5 million). Most of this success was achieved without the aid of cocaine, removed from the drink in 1905.

BAD MEDICINE?

Taking the coke out of Coke must have been a big commercial risk for Candler. The quack market had been awash with products such as Dr Don's Coca, Liebig's Coca Beef Tonic and Kumfort's Cola Extract. Because coca dried up the nasal passages it was mixed with snuff as a cure for hay fever and asthma: the first widespread use of sniffing to get a rush. You could buy wonderfully named preparations such as Dr Tucker's Specific or Anglo-American Catarrh Powder. There were cough drops, toothache remedies, chewing 'paste' (the Inca never got proper credit for that one) and even coca cigarettes 'guaranteed to lift depression'. Cocaine could be bought from chemists as a neat solution or even as pure cocaine hydrochloride or 'powder coke'.

As the market expanded, so the price at first increased. Drugs companies such as Merck in Germany, and Parke-Davis of the USA, saw prices per gram quadruple soon after Koller's discovery, to stand at $13 (£9). It couldn't last. More manufacturers flung themselves on to the bandwagon, there was oversupply and the price dropped. By the late 1880s, cocaine was so common that bar tenders were sprinkling it around liberally, what you might call Scotch with Attitude.

THE MAN WITH THE PLAN

The reason for the explosion in production was simple. In the past the big drugs companies had faced the same problem as the early medical researchers. They couldn't get enough coca leaf. It couldn't be grown in North America or western Europe and exporting bulky good-quality leaves was both expensive and difficult. Parke-Davis decided it needed a man in South America to check out possible new options. It chose Henry Hurd Rusby, recent medical graduate, botanist and, most importantly, a man with a brainwave.

Rusby reasoned that it must be possible to make cocaine on the spot. Trouble was, he didn't have a state-of-the-art pharmaceutical plant handy. He decided to improvise to see if there wasn't an easier, simpler way to produce the drug. The method he hit upon – still essentially the same used in the industry today – involved soaking the leaves in acid, shaking up the muddy brown result in alcohol to extract the alkaloids, adding an alkali like sodium bicarbonate, scooping out the dirty-white paste (known as *pasta basica*, or basic paste) and drying it out. The paste is up to two-thirds pure cocaine, it is compact and easy to transport, and is quickly converted into the final product: cocaine hydrochloride. In Peru, a new cocaine boom was born – 350 years after the Spanish one – in which processing factories as well as coca growers played a key role.

THE DOWNSIDE

Back at Coca-Cola, Candler wasn't so much worried by the competition as the fact that cocaine had side-effects. Side-effects were not good for business, particularly with the media homing in on a scandal. There had been a public relations disaster in 1902 when a court heard disturbing evidence that children were becoming addicted to the drink. Candler was having none of it and ordered cocaine to be removed from the Coke recipe. Meanwhile public unease was heightened by reports of hospital patients suffering from blackouts and convulsions and even dying as they received cocaine anaesthetics.

Health hazards were one thing, but when reports began to filter through of a link to violent crime, the Great American Public took a collective step backwards. The problem was that cocaine had become so easy to find that it was no longer the preserve of the filthy rich. People on limited incomes had got themselves habits they couldn't fund legally. What did they do? According to the government they robbed and stole to buy the drug, and they robbed and stole while they were high.

In March 1911 the head of America's anti-opium campaign, Dr Hamilton Wright, wrote to *The New York*

Times expressing his concern: 'The misuse of cocaine is a direct incentive to crime... It is perhaps of all factors a singular one in augmenting the criminal ranks. The illicit use of the drug is most difficult to cope with and the habitual use of it temporarily raises the power of the criminal to a point where, in resisting arrest, there is no hesitation to murder.'

This was bad enough. Next, some medical journals began reporting that 'the Negroes' in parts of the American South had become addicted to cocaine. Apparently many of them worked long shifts in the New Orleans docks and discovered that a sniff of that magic white powder they regularly unloaded allowed them to work longer and harder on less food. This was obviously fine with the dock management. Soon a vibrant drug market had sprung up, with local plantation workers also getting in on the act. By 1902 *The British Medical Journal* was telling how plantation owners had to issue cocaine rations to keep their men happy.

Soon the newspapers were on the case, with lurid reports of 'coke orgies', rapes and mass murders committed by blacks. One particularly ludicrous account was submitted by a police chief in Asheville, North Carolina, who told how a 'hitherto inoffensive Negro' had been driven mad by cocaine and pulled a knife. The officer placed his revolver over the man's heart and fired. He then fired a second shot into his chest. Neither of these bullets, claimed the cop, had any effect. The only thing that worked was to bludgeon that crazy Negro to death with a club. So he did and promptly headed off to buy a bigger gun.

Not for the first time in the history of this drug – and all drugs – propaganda was accepted as fact.

KICKS FROM COCAINE…

At the end of the 19th century doctors, dentists and chemists accounted for a huge percentage of coke addicts. This was partly because they could get it easily, but they were also curious to check out its effects on themselves. There was a belief, held among some scientists even until the 1980s, that cocaine wasn't really addictive.

True, the early glut of production never developed into a national epidemic, but this wasn't because the drug was benign. The reality is that new US laws were restricting availability – by 1922 dealers risked ten-year prison terms – and the street price was creeping up. Soon, ordinary American users couldn't afford to acquire a habit. Besides, as the 1930s dawned there were cheap new stimulants appearing, which were legal and, apparently, harmless. They were called amphetamines.

The US cocaine market was perhaps ten years ahead of Europe's experience. Cocaine was still widespread in Paris (where half of all prostitutes were rumoured to be users), Barcelona, Madrid, Brussels, Berne and Rome. Germany, the world's biggest producer, had been ordered to cut back under the 1919 Treaty of Versailles, which ended World War I. The

Germans had been stockpiling supplies, however, and in a country economically devastated by war these inevitably filtered on to the black market. People saw coke as a way to escape the national depression. Dealers cashed in, often eking out a stash by mixing in additional impurities.

In London, the *Daily Mail* reported that the drug was widely used among the West End's professional classes (barristers, politicians, actors and showbusiness types). Members of this young, smart and wealthy set were said to meet in designated flats or houses for 'a few doses of cocaine and a night of revelry'. Here was an early sign of the shifting cocaine culture. People began to see it as a drug of the upper classes and the 'gay young things' (that's gay in the traditional sense) of 1920s London. Cocaine was getting arty...and marching upmarket.

A KICK UP THE ARTS

Nowhere was this more obvious than in popular music and literature. One verse of the classic Cole Porter song 'I Get A Kick Out Of You' (covered in the 1980s by Roxy Music) opens with the words: 'I get no kick from cocaine'. After some subtle behind-the-scenes pressure – presumably to prevent apoplexy among conservatives – Porter's version was sometimes reworded 'Some get their perfume from Spain'. At least it rhymed.

The final line of a traditional blues song called 'Cocaine Lil' ran:

They laid her out in her cocaine clothes
She wore a snowbird hat with a crimson rose
And on her tombstone you'll find this refrain
She died as she lived, sniffing cocaine

And then there was the great 1930s blues classic 'Minnie The Moocher', which tells how the heroine 'fell in love with a guy named Smokey – she loved him though he was cokey'.

Fiction writers such as Agatha Christie and Dorothy Sayers both produced stories featuring cocaine addicts. Proust picks up the upper-class theme through his character the Vicomtesse de St Fiarcie, who destroys her good looks through overuse of the drug. The Russian-American novelist Vladimir Nabokov, whose best-known work was *Lolita*, once complained that his editor rejected a short story called 'A Matter Of Chance' on the basis that 'we don't print stories about cocainists'. But the biggest fictional coke addict of the age was none other than the world's greatest detective, that quintessential English hero Sherlock Holmes.

Holmes is first seen dabbling in the drug in *A Scandal In Bohemia*. Dr Watson tells how his friend alternates 'between cocaine and ambition', bizarrely attributing Holmes's drowsiness to his habit. This is probably because the author, Sir Arthur Conan Doyle, was not quite sure what cocaine actually does. He assumed that because it's an anaesthetic it must be a downer.

HIGH IN THE HILLS

Music? Literature? It could only be a matter of time before Hollywood also became a player in the cocaine trade. In the 1920s the emerging film industry with its pantheon of rich, hedonistic celebrities was a lucrative marketplace for cocaine dealers. Americans already perceived movie stars as sex-and-drug crazed ne'er-do-wells and the Fatty Arbuckle scandal of September 1921, in which a young actress called Virginia Rappe died during a hotel party thrown by the silent screen comic, simply reinforced this view. In fact there was no proper evidence against Arbuckle, other than that he had consumed bootlegged drink in breach of Prohibition laws, but the popular press tried and sentenced him, and worked in a cocaine angle for good measure.

In fairness, making a link between Hollywood and cocaine was hardly wide of the mark. Arbuckle worked for Mack Sennett's Keystone Studios along with a young actress called Mabel Normand, who became embroiled in a high-profile murder case. She was ruined after being exposed as a cocaine addict with a truly awesome $2,000-a-month (£1,400) habit. Barbara La Marr, who starred alongside Douglas Fairbanks in his 1921 film *The Three Musketeers*, was said to keep a permanent stash of coke in her grand piano, using it to stay awake 22 hours a day (she later overdosed on heroin).

Good breeding made no difference. The acclaimed American actress Tallulah Bankhead, daughter of

Democratic party leader and House of Representatives speaker William Brockman Bankhead, told in her autobiography how she once mistakenly put cocaine solution in her eyes, mistaking it for eyedrops. When a friend at the New York restaurant urged her to call a doctor, Bankhead threw a wobbly. 'I put the cocaine in my eyes and I don't tell that to doctors or anyone else,' she fumed. She is also, famously, the source of the quip 'Cocaine isn't habit-forming. I should know, I've been using it for years.'

In the eyes of middle-class America, Hollywood was built on 'happy dust' and booze. There was a clampdown by the police and a feeding frenzy among the press, resulting in a marked drop in use. Even so, some stars wouldn't leave cocaine alone. America's first 'drugs tsar', Harry Anslinger, tells in his memoirs of the 'swashbuckling' actor who hawked himself around Europe trying to get the drug from doctors. This star – which only a blind Alaskan hermit would fail to recognize as Errol Flynn – claimed he needed the drug to cure everything from an inferiority complex to painful haemorrhoids. Flynn eventually admitted to Anslinger that he used cocaine to heighten sexual pleasure.

COLOMBIA, COKE CENTRAL
Colombia had a long and lucrative tradition of smuggling, particularly luxury household goods, alcohol and precious stones. It was an undeveloped country with a long, remote coastline and easy access to the Panama Canal free-trade

area. No coca or cocaine had ever been produced there but, hey, so what? If it was valuable and you could smuggle it, you could count the Colombian underworld in. Corruption was rife, drugs law enforcement negligible.

At first the Colombians simply set themselves up as middlemen, servicing both their Cuban and Chilean partners. Then they began to muscle in on their customers' territory, bidding for unrefined coca paste in Bolivia and Peru, cooking it up and distributing it across the USA. By 1970 the Colombian cartels had come from nowhere to challenge Cuban domination. Millions of young Americans revelling in the rebellion culture of the day decided cocaine was the new Big Thing: less dangerous than heroin or speed, more predictable than LSD, more exciting than marijuana and dead simple to take. Besides – and this was the clincher – it was supposed to take sexual orgasm to new heights.

Almost overnight – its image boosted by a plethora of rock songs and films such as *Easy Rider* – cocaine became easily accessible. *Rolling Stone* magazine declared it 'Drug of the Year' for 1970. *Newsweek* famously reported that 'orgasms go better with coke'. Students looking to make their fortunes worked out that you could buy a kilo (2¼lb) in Peru for $4,000 (£2,750), cut it, and sell it back home for $300,000 (£200,000). Oh, and in case there were any doubters one police narcotics chief told how cocaine produced 'a good high... and you don't get hooked'.

THE DRUG LORDS OF COLOMBIA

The 1970s cocaine boom in America coincided with a major shift in production. Chile had always been a major supplier to the USA, but the coup by General Pinochet in 1973 was bad news for traffickers. Literally hundreds were rounded up and despatched on planes to America. It was Pinochet's way of saying thanks to the CIA for helping ease him into power.

Colombian drug barons moved quickly to full the vacuum. They had no shortage of muscle (the country was awash with guns after a civil war) and they were not afraid to use it, especially on foreigners and gringos trying their luck as cocaine smugglers. Soon any serious competition from American gangs was seen off, sometimes violently.

The leading cartels sent representatives to Bolivia and Peru to jack up coca production and ensure a steady supply. They bribed local cops and politicians to stop domestic interference. They also began sounding out Colombian nationals resident in America to see if anyone fancied making an easy buck as a distributor. The ex-pats usually did. Ever since Colombia's textile industry went belly-up in the 1960s there has been a steady stream of emigrants seeking a new life in the US of A. Unfortunately, that new life was uncannily similar to the old one: namely poverty and unemployment. For these people cocaine was a way out. They were well-placed to co-ordinate supply.

By the mid-1970s the minor players in Colombia had fallen by the wayside, often quite literally, courtesy of 100 rounds or so from a machine pistol. There was vicious fighting between the Colombians and the Cubans (the latter coming a distinct second) but DEA agents noted with interest that there was not always all-out war between the big cartels. On the contrary, they sometimes struck alliances, combining shipments to share profits and swapping intelligence to guard against informers. The cities of Medellín and Cali became the centre of the cocaine business. Each had their own, notorious drug families.

In Cali, names in the frame included Helmer 'Pacho' Herrera, Jose Santacruz-Londono and several members of the Rodriguez-Orejuela clan. In Medellín one of the first high-profile gangsters was a former prostitute called Griselda Blanco, aka the Black Widow (on account of her three husbands who had been killed in drug wars). Her other nicknames included the Godmother, La Gaga (the Stutterer) and Muneca (Dollface).

GRISELDA BLANCO

In 1979 Blanco was the best-known – and most feared – cocaine trafficker in the United States. Then aged 36, she had transferred the hub of her operation to Miami. She was attractive, flamboyant and tried to work wherever possible with other women, especially widows. Drug folklore has it that she even designed her own knickers with hidden pockets suitable for carrying coke stashes through customs.

Her gang was known as Los Pistoleros and she had several hundred names on her payroll. These hitmen were credited with inventing a crude, but effective, assassination method in which a motorcycle driver and pillion passenger would draw alongside their target car in a busy city street. The pillion man would then empty his machine pistol into the occupants and the pair would hightail it through traffic queues. But let it not be said that Blanco's killers were unimaginative. One was rumoured to tape shut the eyes and mouths of his victims, drain off their blood in the bath and neatly fold remaining skin and bone into old TV or hi-fi boxes.

Soon the DEA and the DAS (Colombia's equivalent of the FBI) were watching other major drug lords. There was Jorge Luis Ochoa Vasquez (the Fat Man), Jose Gonzalo Rodriguez Gacha (the Mexican), an underworld enforcer whose hobbies were – in order – violence, soccer (as in buying teams) and horses. There was the legendary Caribbean drug transporter known as Carlos Lehder. And then there was El Padrino (the Godfather), otherwise known as Pablo Escobar Gaviria. Together, these four were the brains behind the notorious Medellín cartel.

The DAS knew that rival traffickers would occasionally blow each other away, although they had no real conception of the term 'cocaine wars' until 22 November 1975 when air-traffic controllers at Cali spotted a light plane trying to land under cover of the radar clutter surrounding an Avianca Airlines commercial flight. Police arrested the two pilots and recovered 600kg (1,320lbs) of cocaine, then the biggest seizure on record. There was mayhem on the streets, with 40 gangsters wiped out in a single weekend. Curiously, all the killings were in Medellín rather than Cali. Medellín was declared cocaine capital of the world.

EL PADRINO

The Medellín bosses were all ruthless, murdering, millionaire villains, but history will record Escobar (El Padrino, the Godfather) as the most successful. In fact, he was arguably the greatest criminal the world has seen. Born into a middle-class background (his mother was a teacher and his father a farmer) he left high school with enough wit and intelligence to run a legitimate business. Instead he started work as a hi-fi smuggler's enforcer and graduated to kidnapping (a growth industry in 1970s Colombia).

When in 1976 he was arrested in possession of 39kg (86lb) of coke the DAS believed he was merely a drug 'mule' or delivery man. This view rapidly changed. First, Escobar's arrest order was mysteriously revoked. Then the head of the DAS got a death threat. The two arresting cops were murdered along with their regional commander. The judge who ordered the arrest was murdered. A newspaper editor who wrote the story eight years later was murdered and his newspaper bombed. The moral of this tale? Don't bust Pablo Escobar Gaviria.

By the turn of the 1980s Escobar was wallowing in money.

A cool $500,000 (£345,000) per day according to some estimates, rising to $1 million (£700,000) a day by the mid-1980s. These kind of sums are not easy to spend but Pablo did his best. He bought 2,800ha (7,000 acres) of land east of Medellín, built a luxurious ranch complete with swimming pools and, obviously, mortar emplacements, and hung a Piper Cub light aeroplane above the entrance gate. Everybody knew, especially the drug agents, that this was the plane in which he had flown his first cocaine shipment to America.

Escobar didn't stop there. He bought dozens of wild animals, turned them loose in the ranch grounds and opened the place as a public zoo. He became Public Benefactor No.1 by building 500 houses in Medellín and giving them to poor families. He mended roads, built churches, wired in street lamps, paid for food wagons to tour poor estates and ensured that the residents got free private healthcare. Every year, at Christmas, he handed out 5,000 toys to underprivileged children. He even formed his own political party, called Civismo en Marcha (Good Citizenship on the March). In 1982 he got himself elected as a member of the Colombian parliament, a position that, under the constitution, guaranteed him immunity from prosecution.

JORGE OCHOA

That same year Colombia was reeling under a new threat from a revolutionary Marxist group calling itself M-19. It was raising cash for the cause through kidnapping and on 12

November 1981 its terrorists abducted Marta Nieves Ochoa from outside Medellín's Antioquia University. This was a bad mistake. It was one thing to target industrialists and politicians. It was quite another to lift one of the five Ochoa sisters. Jorge Ochoa was suitably unimpressed and, within a couple of weeks, a summit of all the major drug cartels had formed a vigilante group known as Muerte a Secuestradores (MAS) (Death to Kidnappers).

Three weeks after Marta's kidnap, a light aeroplane banked gently over a crowded football stadium in Cali and dropped some leaflets announcing that 233 'businessmen' had formed the MAS to stamp out kidnapping. The wording of the leaflet suggested that Jorge and his mates weren't messing about: 'The basic objective will be the public and immediate execution of all those involved in kidnappings beginning from the date of this communiqué ... [they] will be hung from the trees in public parks or shot and marked with the sign of our group – MAS.'

The statement warned that jailed kidnappers would be murdered or, if this proved impossible, 'retribution will fall on their comrades in jail and on their closest family members'.

Within six weeks 100 M-19 members had been captured and handed over to the police. No one knows precisely how many were murdered, but judging by the speed with which Marta was freed, M-19 was clearly anxious to end this little spat. The word on the street was that the Ochoa family never did pay the $12 million (£8.3 million) ransom.

It looked as though Escobar, Jorge Ochoa et al were the unofficial rulers of Colombia. With their private armies and huge resources they feared no one. Occasionally there was an inter-gang feud but nothing they couldn't handle. As for the government, its efforts at drug control were barely even irritating.

ENTER THE ENFORCERS

Until, that is, in August 1983, when newly elected president Belisario Betancur appointed a determined young congressman called Lara Bonilla as his Minister of Justice. Bonilla recognized that drug money was destroying his country's economy because it required a vast black market to prosper. He began by asking awkward questions: how did Colombia's mega-millionaires make their money? Why did they need all those aeroplanes? Escobar's people tried bribes to keep him quiet, then death threats. But it made no difference; Bonilla publicly branded Escobar a trafficker and ordered his chief of police Jaime Ramirez to bust every cocaine laboratory in the country.

Ramirez was a rare jewel in Colombian law-enforcement circles. He was incorruptible. So when in 1984 he was informed by the DEA of a major cocaine plant deep in the Colombian jungle he organized an attack so secret that none of the police and army officers knew where they were going until they were actually in the air.

The DEA's intelligence was spot on, not least because their undercover people had sold a huge consignment of anhydrous ethyl ether – a key ingredient of the cocaine production process – to a Medellín cartel representative called Frank Torres. In with the ether barrels were some satellite beacons, and soon the DEA was analysing satellite photos of a 1km (0.6 mile) airstrip in the middle of nowhere. The photos didn't need much analysis. Neither did the amount of radio traffic beaming out of the place.

The lab was called Tranquilandia and once the Colombian SWAT team had seen off its guards they knew they had hit the mother lode. It looked like something from a James Bond set: a huge complex with quarters for guards, chemists, pilots and cooks; there were hot showers, flushing toilets, mains electricity and weapons stores; and everywhere lay thousands upon thousands of chemical drums. One logbook showed the place had processed 15 tonnes/tons of cocaine paste in January and February that year.

Ramirez's men also found a pilot's notebook containing a convenient map of labs in the area with radio frequencies. Over the next few days the raiders visited each of them: Cocolandia, where a tonne/ton of the drug was wrapped in waterproof packaging; Cocolandia 2 (500kg/1,100lb); Tranquilandia 2 (4 tonnes/tons); El Diamante (half a tonne/ton). Over the next fortnight Ramirez recovered 8,500kg (18,700lb) of pure cocaine and 1,500kg (3,300lb) of cocaine base. He seized seven planes, nine labs and

12,000 chemical drums. The whole shooting match was worth over $1 billion (£0.7 billion). Even by Medellín standards this was serious spondulicks.

Lara Bonilla rightly took the credit for the operation. He also knew he was a dead man walking. He told a journalist friend that he would be killed on 30 April 1984 and, sure enough, that afternoon two young hitmen hired by the cartel roared alongside his official car on a Yamaha motorbike – in classic Los Pistoleros style – and sprayed the back seat with bullets. Lara's bodyguards opened up immediately, killing one and injuring the other. But it was too late. Colombia had lost the one man truly capable of striking back at the drug lords.

President Betancur responded in a national radio broadcast at 3am the following morning. He described the drugs business as the most serious problem in Colombian history and pledged a 'war without quarter' against traffickers. Escobar and his friends weren't unduly worried. They'd heard this kind of stuff before. But Bonilla's memorial service wiped the smiles off their faces. During his address Betancur announced that, 'Colombia will hand over criminals wanted in other countries so that they may be punished as an example.' He got a standing ovation from the congregation.

Reintroducing extradition was a brave move. Escobar, Ochoa and their lieutenants knew that if ever they got hauled before an American court they would never taste freedom again. Bribes and escape plots would be useless. So, like

Betancur, the Medellín cartel also prepared for war without quarter. The result was an unprecedented level of bombings and killings on the streets, an increasing cycle of violence in which American diplomats, DEA officers and their families also became prime targets.

The country was now quite literally a war zone. At one point, anti-tank rockets were fired at the US Embassy and government tanks were deployed to end an M-19 terrorist siege at Bogotá's Palace of Justice. Almost 150 people died in the subsequent shoot-out. Judges, journalists and their families were threatened or murdered, and in 1986 the main cause of death for adult males in Colombia was not heart disease or cancer but murder. Shootings in Medellín alone were reported at an average of almost ten per day. In 1988 and 1989 it is estimated that death squads accounted for 40,000 citizens. And amid all this death and destruction, the Medellín and Cali cartels began fighting a turf war.

For the Colombian government the killing was too high a price. Extradition had to end. In 1990, after an election campaign in which three presidential candidates were murdered, Liberal Party leader César Gaviria Trujillo, was elected. Two months later his new constitution banned the extradition of Colombian citizens and Gaviria offered an amnesty to drug traffickers who turned themselves in. Pablo Escobar was among those who obliged.

He was sent to prison to await trial. But it was a funny kind of prison because, well, Pablo owned it. There was a health club, a marijuana plot, a disco, a motorbike scrambling track, chalets for entertaining women visitors – even an underground bombproof bunker. The prison 'cells' all had videos, TVs and hi-fis. Escobar had the telephones and fax lines he needed to run his business, and enjoyed the occasional trip to a soccer match – under police escort, of course. It was all quite hunky-dory, until he got too cocksure.

Perhaps to emphasize that he was still in charge, Escobar tortured and killed two former associates who had been trying to negotiate a reduction on the monthly $1 million (£700,000) 'tax' he'd levied on their cocaine trafficking. The police decided this was too much. Pablo should go to a proper prison. Inevitably, though, he was tipped off and in July 1992 simply discharged himself. He went into hiding in the heart of Medellín, moving from house to house and communicating from moving cars to prevent his phone calls being traced.

Had he not ordered those last two gangland killings he might have pulled it off. But now even Pablo's own people feared he was going insane. They wondered if he would turn on them next and some key aides defected to the Cali cartel – then headed by Pacho Herrera and the Rodriguez-Orejuela brothers – for protection. Now Escobar had not only the DAS, DEA and CIA after him but a new organization called Los PEPES (People Persecuted by Pablo Escobar). It was run by the Cali boys.

By November police mobile tracking units had pinpointed Escobar's phone calls to a 200 sq m (2,000 sq ft) area of the city. It was far too densely populated to surround, so they played a waiting game hoping his guard would slip. On 2 December it did. He stayed put rather than talk on the move and he spoke for six minutes, long enough to get a secure signal fix. Then he was seen at a window and commando-trained police moved in. Pablo was not the kind of guy to be taken alive. And he wasn't.

Escobar is now a distant memory, yet for Colombia's new cocaine kings the past decade has been business as usual. When you hear politicians talk of the 'war on drugs' they usually forget to mention that it's a war that patently isn't being won. Certainly not by destroying coca fields or raiding traffickers. Not by prosecuting dodgy chemical manufacturers and money launderers. Not by busting backstreet labs and dealers. Deep down, law enforcement agencies know and privately accept this. The cocaine trade abhors a vacuum and there'll always be someone willing to blow in and make a fortune. In reality, all the cops can do is make life tough for the bad guys.

Cocaine will always be in circulation. The question is, will it be in your circulation?

COCAINE, SEX AND THE FEEL-GOOD FACTOR

If you've ever had a sexual orgasm you'll know how wonderful it feels. That's because your unconscious brain regards the reproductive act as the single most important thing you can do with your life. Forget global warming, democracy, human rights, scientific discovery, justice, racial equality and all the other great issues of the day. As far as your brain is concerned, pal, your number one duty is to get laid.

Unless, of course, you are a regular cocaine user.

BETTER THAN SEX…

Dr Bill Jacobs, assistant professor of addiction medicine at Florida University's Department of Psychiatry, explains it like this: 'When you take cocaine you create an artificial stimulus to your brain's reward pathway. The pathway is there to keep our species alive: it's food, water, nurturing the young and especially sex. These are all natural rewards which turn on the reward pathways and tell us, "You did good, do that again."

'If those natural rewards turn on the pathway to a value of one, well, cocaine turns it on to a value of 1,000. That is just not a natural phenomenon. Our brains are not made to run like that. When you remove the cocaine you immediately start to fall from a much higher place.'

Aidan Gray, national co-ordinator for the UK charity Conference on Crack and Cocaine (COCA), describes the buzz in more colloquial terms. The former drug-project worker has specialized in cocaine since 1994 and is among Europe's leading authorities on its effects.

'Is cocaine an aphrodisiac? I'm not sure that's the right word. It certainly does increase anticipation and if you've ever been to a theme park like Disneyland and you're waiting for the big ride you'll know that sense of "Ohmigod! What am I doing?" That's your fight or flight response. It's where craving comes from. It's your heart beating, the funny churning in your stomach, the sweating – all that stuff. It is rooted in anticipation. Like at school when you have a first date with someone you really fancy, there's that strange giddy feeling. Anticipation and sex are very closely linked.

'The other connection is the brain's pleasure-giving neurotransmitters. There's a definite tick alongside cocaine's effect on dopamine and a lot of scientists think seratonin is also a factor. Cocaine works on reward. When you have lunch and you enjoy it you get a small release of neurotransmitters and that reinforces your behaviour. Your brain knows that eating is good for you.

'The biggest high from your brain's neurotransmitters is meant to be sex. That's your orgasm. When you are taking cocaine you are leap-frogging way over that. The brain mechanisms are very similar for sex and coke. So when you combine a sexual partner, a gram or two and perhaps a bottle of champagne you can see why people think there is an aphrodisiac effect. The pleasure is both physical and neurological.'

Dopamine, seratonin – let's face it, these aren't names to concentrate your mind as you snort a line or achieve sexual ecstasy (unless you are an unbelievably sad person). But neurotransmitters seem to be at the core of cocaine addiction, and the reason why taking the drug is so much fun. Thanks to scientists such as Dr Nora Volkow, we now know a lot more about them.

ALL IN THE MIND?

During studies at the University of Texas, Houston, in 1984 Volkow noticed that the brains of cocaine users showed severe changes. She began photographing them using a positron emission tomography scanner, a process that involves tagging molecules with radioactive particles (positrons), injecting them into the blood and monitoring their voyage around the brain. She quickly discovered that cocaine has a special relationship with neurotransmitters such as dopamine.

First, what's a neurotransmitter? Imagine the wiring in your house. You switch on a light and because this completes an electrical circuit, the bulb is powered into life. Your brain also uses electrical circuits but it doesn't mess about with cumbersome physical connections. Instead it completes circuits by sending chemicals – neurotransmitters – from one nerve cell to another. This happens almost instantaneously. Neurotransmitters make your body perform physical functions – talking, sneezing, cutting toenails – but they also handle emotion and instinct for survival. Eating chocolate, taking a hot shower, drinking ice-cold beer in a heatwave, cuddling your kids and (especially) having sex: dopamine makes all these experiences feel good for various evolutionary reasons.

Dopamine messengers are being released into synapses (the spaces between nerve cells) all the time. But they don't hang around because your brain immediately sends out transporters to round them up and shepherd them back to their cells ready for next time. This is called re-uptake. If it didn't happen, your orgasm would last all afternoon and disturb your post-coital nap.

Cocaine uses sneaky tactics to disrupt this mechanism. It attaches itself to perhaps two-thirds of your dopamine transporters and disables them. The stranded dopamine keeps swirling around the spaces, or synapses, between nerve cells, and does its genetic duty by dispensing euphoric joy. That's your cocaine high and it will last for between 40 and 60 minutes, depending on the method of consumption.

What happens then is unpleasant. After attaching itself to a dopamine transporter the cocaine detaches fairly quickly (although traces remain in the brain for two to three days). If no more arrives the dopamine is duly rounded up, except now the process becomes much more rigorous. It's as though the brain is a fussy mother, angry that her kids have been out too long. Dopamine levels fall below normal – below the level they existed prior to cocaine intake – and, sure enough, that's your crash. The immediate urge is to take more cocaine, to 'binge' until either supplies run out or exhaustion takes over.

All this happens within your medial forebrain bundle, the structures of which are your frontal cortex, nucleus accumbens and ventral tegmental area. Most recent research has focused on what happens when dopamine leaves the ventral tegmental area and heads for the nucleus accumbens. In this area of the brain lie the roots of addiction. Scientists can argue about whether it's a physical or psychological addiction, but addiction it is. When you take cocaine regularly your brain physically alters.

The most obvious change is a drop in the number of dopamine receptors on nerve cells. With fewer receptors, those nerves are denied normal levels of stimulation and so pleasurable experiences other than cocaine no longer induce familiar feelings of 'natural' happiness. This is why some of Aidan Gray's clients preferred coke to sex.

For reasons not fully understood it seems that taking cocaine irregularly may sensitize some people (they become more responsive to the same dose). But regular use leads to tolerance and so more of the drug is needed to reach the same level as a previous high. Evidence suggests that, for regular users, dopamine receptors become permanently damaged and the brain never manages to restore them to pre-cocaine levels. This creates a huge problem for those seeking treatment because their desire for the drug is never quite diminished. They remember it as the only thing that delivered true pleasure. The best they can hope for is to resist their craving until enough dopamine receptors come back into play, allowing other things in life to feel pleasurable again.

According to Dr Volkow, the bingeing tendency may be caused by cocaine's ability to dabble in other areas of the brain, specifically the bits that tell us when we've had enough. This is our 'satiety' response. Volkow believes that in switching it off, cocaine ensures that users binge even though they know they will suffer at the end of it.

'Pleasure is a natural reinforcer to increase the probability that a species will engage in a given behaviour and continue that behaviour,' she told a National Institute on Drug Abuse research briefing in July 1998. 'Once these urges have been satisfied the body's normal response is satiety or "that's enough". When satiety is suppressed, the pleasurable properties of cocaine serve as a trigger for activating brain pathways that will then maintain the drug-consuming behaviour.'

Cocaine experiments on animals support this view, even though the behaviour of caged creatures is unlikely to mirror that of free human beings. In the 1960s researchers gave one group of laboratory rats unlimited access to heroin while another group got unlimited coke. Heroin is a sedative or 'downer' and so these rats tended to sleep more. Their consumption became routine and regulated. The cocaine rats on the other hand didn't stop self-administering hits until they became physically exhausted. They didn't sleep or eat and after waking from a collapsed state they immediately took more of the drug. They were all dead inside a month. The heroin rats by this time had developed a habit, yet groomed, slept and ate fairly normally.

There are plenty more examples of animal experiments that demonstrate cocaine's extraordinary power over brain function. In one case a chimp was trained to hit a bar to receive a single dose of coke. Once he'd worked this out, researchers began increasing the number of times he needed to hit the bar to get the same dose. The aim was to measure the addictive potential of the drug and scientists assumed there would come a point where the chimp had to press the bar so many times for his fix that he'd get bored and find something else to do. He didn't. They stopped the experiment after he pressed the bar 12,800 times for a single shot: 100 – 1,600 per cent more than for any other drug.

WHAT'S THE CRACK?

Ever wondered why you can't get hooked on nicotine quit-smoking patches? Why no one ever pleads with their neighbourhood pharmacist for 'just one more patch' to get through the day. After all, this is the same drug smoked by billions; the drug that is so seductive when inhaled. A patch contains as much as a few cigarettes. How come nicotine hooks you one way but not the other?

It's simple. The reason people like recreational drugs is that they crank up the pleasure centre of the brain. The more drugs you take the greater the pleasure rush, at least up to the point where you overdose. But, more importantly, it's the speed with which these drugs hit the brain that really counts. If you inhale them they go straight into your main blood vessels and you're in the fast lane to Pleasure City. If you snort, drink, eat or 'patch' them, then they have to trog around the back roads of your circulatory system before they find the freeway. The eventual rush will be more gradual and less intense, although it'll last longer.

This is the essential difference between a patch and a cigarette. It's also the difference between snorting powder coke and smoking crack cocaine. Because the high is more intense there's a powerful incentive to light up again as soon as the (equally intense) crash takes over. But before we tell the story of crack we need to know more about its parentage. That means a trip back to the

1970s and the amazing new wonder drug of America's *Easy Rider* generation. Cocaine freebase.

FANCY FREEBASE?

When you sniff cocaine you're actually consuming cocaine hydrochloride (or cocaine salt). The production process for this has essentially remained the same since a young student called Albert Niemann discovered it while working at the University of Gottingen in 1859. Niemann washed coca leaves in alcohol and sulphuric acid, distilled off the alcohol and separated out a resin, which he shook with bicarbonate of soda. This substance was again distilled to produce the now familiar, rod-shaped white crystals.

A quarter of a century later, drugs companies discovered a simpler method, which could be carried out on-site in South America's coca plantations (avoiding the problems associated with exporting fast-rotting coca leaves). They dowsed leaves in acid, shook up the sludgy result with alcohol, added a strong alkali such as bicarbonate of soda and, hey presto!, basic paste or *pasta basica*. This is between 40 and 65 per cent pure and is still the form most favoured by traffickers. It is a rough mixture of contaminated cocaine compounds, which is designed to be further refined into cocaine hydrochloride higher up the trading chain. As paste it can be smoked because it vaporizes quickly when heated. Ordinary powder coke just degrades. Light it and you might as well burn money.

Now the freebase story gets a tad speculative and confusing. According to the world's leading authority on the history of cocaine science, the University of California's Professor Ron Siegel, here's what probably happened.

Around 1970 a pioneering American cocaine trafficker in Peru notices production workers puffing away at something they call base. He tries it, likes it and, back in the USA, he smokes a bit of his usual cocaine hydrochloride mixed with tobacco. But something is wrong. There's no big rush. So he calls a friend with some chemistry know-how and asks why base might be different. They check out a textbook and discover the definition of a chemical 'base'.

They establish that cocaine hydrochloride (cocaine salt) can easily be converted back to base form by removing the hydrochloride molecule. This involves adding a strong alkali and dissolving everything in a solvent, such as ether. The ether stage is a bit dodgy because the fumes ignite so easily, but once the cocaine dries and crystallizes out it's in a stable form ready for smoking. The amateur chemists call this 'freeing the base' or freebasing.

Their one error is to assume that what the Indians call base and what their textbook calls base are one and the same. Not so. What they end up smoking is close to pure cocaine, not some mishmash of coke-plus-impurities. In drinking terms it's the difference between a light beer and a similar quantity of 90-per-cent-proof Polish vodka. In other words, completely different.

By then, users and scientists alike had realised that freebase was a new phenomenon. Smokers developed bizarre traits, such as constantly staring at the floor searching for a mislaid bit of base. When sharing a pipe they would bicker like children over sweets. Siegel's book *Intoxication* tells how he usually had to provide lab monkeys with a reward to persuade them to smoke drugs. With freebase they needed no reward. One monkey would even try to lick the smoke she exhaled. When Siegel conducted tests on men who had never smoked freebase they spontaneously ejaculated, even though their penises were flaccid. Euphoria was being redefined.

Some cocaine dealers, such as the notorious Ricky Ross – aka Freeway Rick – of South Central, Los Angeles, began offering clients prepared freebase to save them the trouble of cooking up powder coke. Because freebase comes in chunks, and because Ross had natural marketing flair, he called his product Ready Rock. When demand went ballistic he bought and converted houses into fully equipped freebase factories. In 1982 he was processing 15kg (33lb) per week. Two years later production hit 50kg (110lb) per week. As his buying power increased, so the price plummeted: from $25,000 (£17,250) down to a low of $9,500 (£6,500) per kilo (2¼lb). From being an expensive, white middle-class kind of drug, freebase was suddenly available to poorer Hispanic and black communities. At his peak, Ross cleared profits of $100,000 (£70,000) a day.

As the *Los Angeles Times* reported on 20 December 1994, 'If there was an eye of the storm, if there was a criminal mastermind...if there was one outlaw capitalist most responsible for flooding LA's streets with mass-marketed cocaine, his name was Freeway Rick.'

There was another factor, though, for which Ross couldn't take the rap. As more people became familiar with freebase so they experimented with new ways to prepare it. Soon cooks discovered a method that avoided fiddling with beakers and dodging ether fireballs. They just heated ordinary coke powder in a solution with baking soda until the water evaporated. Dead easy. When this type of freebase was lit and smoked it made a crackling sound. If you were a drug dealer what street name would you have come up with?

AMERICA GETS CRACKING

On 17 November 1985, *The New York Times* told the world: 'Three teenagers have sought treatment already this year...for cocaine dependence resulting from the use of a new form of the drug called "crack", or rock-like pieces of prepared freebase.' The media descended like vultures. Rightly or wrongly, 'crack' became the hyped-up horror story of the 1980s.

According to Dr David Smith at the Haight-Ashbury Free Clinic: 'When you snort cocaine you are actually snorting cocaine hydrochloride. With freebase you have an extraction process in which you "basefy" the drug, that is, you extract the hydrochloride using an organic solvent and you dry it. This lowers the vaporization point. When people talk about smoking cocaine what they really mean is vaporizing it. When you freebase, you heat the drug, vaporize it, inhale and you get a blood and brain level similar to an injection.

'With crack it's all pre-prepared. You don't extract it yourself or do any of that. The supplier mixes it with baking soda, which is the base, puts it in the microwave and then cracks off pieces – they call them rocks – to sell. That's one explanation for the drug's name. The other is that it crackles when you smoke it. Either way, it's the fast food of drug culture.

'The analogy I use sounds very simplistic but it gets the message through. Freebase is like a barbecue party. You have your barbecue pit and you go get a bun and a burger, you get all your condiments lined up and all your cooking utensils, and away you go. That's the kind of ritual the middle and upper classes follow.

'Crack cocaine is like going out for a McDonald's takeaway burger. It costs a lot less and it's all pre-prepared. We saw the crack-cocaine epidemic explode and it moved immediately into the lower socio-economic non-white populations. It was no longer a drug of the white middle class but of the lower-class black culture.

'With crack you buy a rock for $20 (£14) and away you go. It's a street drug and you can easily carry it around.

With freebase you've got to have all the equipment – which means paying out around $100 (£70) – and it requires a lot more skill. You have to be careful that you don't produce something that will make you lose perspective and burn yourself up like Richard Pryor.

'Crack has become very much a contributor to sexually transmitted diseases because of the prostitutes, the so-called "crack whores". They use crack cocaine repeatedly to the point that they are offering sex for a rock. They are in a cycle of drug use that, for many, is impossible to break.'

One Miami, Florida, user four months into treatment agreed to explain the lure of the drug. He was in real estate, young, wealthy and a former powder coke user. A business acquaintance showed him how to heat crack on aluminium foil and inhale the fumes.

'If you haven't experienced crack you can't know what ultimate pleasure feels like,' he said. 'It goes beyond any other human experience; you can't even begin to compare it to an orgasm. The first couple of minutes are a new level of consciousness. Your senses are alive in a way you cannot understand.

'After this you get maybe 10 to 15 minutes of feel-good feeling. Then you start to come down and it's a heavy down. You feel depressed big-time, tired and anxious. You know that the quickest way to deal with it is to smoke more crack and so that's what you do. And gradually the highs don't seem quite so high but the lows just keep getting lower. I did this on and off for six months and I was spending God knows how many hundreds of dollars. But at the time I wouldn't have said I was addicted.'

A GUIDE TO THE SIDE-EFFECTS

The side-effects of cocaine fall into short- and long-term categories. Each of these can be subdivided into psychological and physiological effects. Sources for the information outlined below include America's National Institute on Drug Abuse (NIDA) website and Dr Mark Gold MD, distinguished professor at the University of Florida Brain Institute and a leading authority on addiction medicine (from both personal interview and published papers). While this section isn't really intended as 'A Spotter's Guide to Coke-heads', concerned friends and parents of users may find it helpful.

POSSIBLE SHORT-TERM PHYSICAL AND PHYSIOLOGICAL EFFECTS

- A tendency to become talkative and energetic
- An apparent heightening of the senses, particularly sight, sound and touch
- A decreased need for food, water or sleep
- Dilated pupils, constricted blood vessels (the anaesthetic effect) increased temperature, blood pressure and heart rate
- Nausea, headaches and sweating
- Chest pain and breathing difficulties

- Urinary and bowel delay
- Large amounts (eg several hundred milligrams) can trigger onset of tremors, vertigo, muscle twitching
- Large amounts – regardless of whether snorted, smoked or injected – can lead to acute overdose effects such as heart seizures and strokes

POSSIBLE LONG-TERM PHYSICAL AND PHYSIOLOGICAL EFFECTS

- Damage to the nasal septum, causing nosebleeds, sense of smell loss and the 'cocaine sniff'
- Total destruction of the septum (single-nostril syndrome)
- Irregular heartbeat – leading to heart attack (rare); caused by increased oxygen demand on the heart (stimulant effect) and decreased oxygen flow to the heart (blood vessel constriction)
- Temporary paralysis of a limb
- Aortic dissection – the lining of the major vessel carrying blood from the heart tears under increased blood pressure
- Burst blood vessel in the brain (stroke) caused by increased blood pressure
- Overcompensation for the anaesthetizing effect on vocal chords, causing permanent hoarseness
- Bulging eyes; gaunt appearance
- Heart valve disease (linked to needle users)
- 'Black lung' and severe phlegm (crack smoking)
- Increased risk of HIV/hepatitis C (see below)

POSSIBLE SHORT-TERM PSYCHOLOGICAL EFFECTS

- Intense euphoria, sense of well-being, total control over destiny – the 'Superman Syndrome'
- Increased libido (low doses)
- Decreased problem-solving ability
- Restlessness, irritability, vertigo and suspicion of others
- A sense of doom and being out of control (during the crash); feelings of anxiety and panic
- Obsessive behaviour – eg crack smokers picking at scabs or hunting for cocaine fragments

POSSIBLE LONG-TERM PSYCHOLOGICAL EFFECTS

- Coke 'bugs' – a form of cocaine toxosis in which the sufferer believes insects or snakes are crawling beneath his/her skin
- Hallucinations
- Dulling of emotions and feelings of 'natural' pleasure
- Intense paranoia; a mistrust even of family and friends
- Feelings of isolation
- Suicidal thinking and behaviour
- Feelings of impending death
- An (unproven) link to Parkinson's disease

SNIFFING OUT THE STATISTICS

In looking over this list it seems incredible that the 'cocaine is safe' lobby ever gets taken seriously. Measured in the numbers of deaths, you could perhaps argue that the drug has a low mortality risk (which is not the same thing at all), but official drug-related death statistics don't paint the full picture.

In America, hospital emergency room deaths linked to cocaine are running at around 10 per 1,000, a figure that has remained fairly constant for a decade. In Britain, however, the number of cocaine-related deaths has risen alarmingly from 19 in 1995 to 87 in 1999. Is this because there were more users? Are post-mortem detection techniques better? Are coroners being more forthright in their conclusions? At the University of Florida's Brain Institute, Dr Mark Gold believes cocaine death rates are a poor indicator of the true problem.

'When you look at coroners' reports they often don't tell you precisely what the person died of,' he said. 'Maybe they want to protect the family, sometimes they don't have the right tests to make a diagnosis absolutely and other times they just don't bother reporting the detail at all.

'I'm sure there are people around who'll say that powder cocaine isn't really a problem. It would be very hard to find a professor in any faculty in the United States who agrees with that. If you look at the people who smoke and inject cocaine, they started by doing something. We've seen people here who have become addicted to drinking cocaine as a means of weight loss.

'That doesn't mean everyone becomes addicted. Nonetheless, the problems associated with this drug are very great. We've all heard stories of grandmothers who smoked for 80 years and never got lung cancer so it doesn't surprise me that people come up with single-case studies to show that cocaine is really OK.

'Here we have a drug which can hijack the brain, which in essence creates itself as the new drive state. Most experts would say that, particularly when smoked, its specific interaction with the reward circuitry is both unique and compelling. This is why when they take it people feel great, powerful, omnipotent, like the typical laws of nature don't apply to them. If you accept the original dopamine hypothesis you'd say that in the cascade of brain rewards cocaine comes closest to the endgame. It's the ultimate reward.'

He points out that the long-term effects of the drug are poorly understood. Heart problems, heart attacks and strokes are all under suspicion, but suspicion and proof occupy different medical galaxies. Even tobacco has only relatively recently been branded harmful by the Surgeon General – 300 years after it arrived in Europe. Gold says that the most common cause of strokes in young people used to be tumours and 'arterial venous malformations'. Now, according to new British research, the commonest causes are cocaine, amphetamines and ecstasy.

'We need more long-term research,' he said. 'Medicines are viewed by everyone as dangerous until proven absolutely and completely safe and effective. And so we let the pharmaceutical companies and governmental agencies do extensive tests. Everyone complains about how long this takes but you do need 10 or 20 years to bring a drug to market.

'Then you have the drugs of abuse, which are viewed by many as safe until proven dangerous. With cocaine there's no silver bullet to treat addiction. Some groups are looking at vaccines and we've been trying a pharmacological approach without great success. We've also treated addicts who are health professionals – doctors, nurses and the like – and in that setting we use group therapy and support. But if you compare the doctor who's an alcoholic with the doctor who's a cocaine addict, the outcome for the cocaine addict is worse.'

LOOKING FOR A CURE

The quest for a cocaine cure has made some progress. NIDA researchers have focused on dopamine, seratonin and another neurotransmitter – norepinephrine – to produce genetic clones of their various transporters. The hope is that drugs can be designed to chemically alter transporters so that they resist the attachment of cocaine molecules. This would prevent the euphoria of a coke rush. Another idea is to disrupt the mechanisms of cocaine and neutralize it in the blood before it even reaches the brain.

Alternative therapy is also making a case. A study of auricular acupuncture at Yale University, published in the *Archives Of Internal Medicine* journal (August 2000), involved the insertion of needles into the outer ears of 82 volunteer addicts. The group was treated for 45 minutes five times a week and, after two months, was tested for cocaine use. More than half the patients returned negative urine samples compared to 23 per cent and 9.1 per cent in two control groups.

Until a major breakthrough comes, most recovering addicts will have to make do with antidepressants and one-step-at-a-time group therapy similar to the process endured by alcoholics. The essence is to concentrate on avoiding cocaine for a day at a time – even ten minutes at a time – and to reject thoughts of tomorrow. Isolation from cocaine-taking friends and old haunts is key to the strategy because any reminder of coke can trigger its craving.

THE UNPALATABLE FACTS

'When you're taking a drug you never want to understand the full consequences and dangers involved,' says Aidan Gray of COCA. 'It's pissing on the bonfire, it spoils the high. There's this strong image that powder coke is OK, it's pure, it's fine, but there's also this thing about the word "cocaine". I've come across people saying, "I just take cocaine. I don't do crack." Very often they are playing with words.

'There are a number of dance clubs where people openly do crack and freebase. Everyone calls it cocaine and technically, of course, they're right, it is. That's the term they've learnt. But this group is not getting any attention from drug agencies and neither are they getting independent information. I've worked exclusively with cocaine users longer than most professionals in this country – since 1994 – and what I've come across is incredible ignorance. There's been a load of initiatives in the UK on the dangers of heroin, safer use, all that kind of stuff. But there's been nothing like that for crack and cocaine.'

Gray's comments have massive implications for cocaine users everywhere. Over the years part of the drug's appeal has been that it is quick, clean and simple to take. In contrast, the AIDS epidemic has reinforced perceptions that needles represent a seedy, dangerous lifestyle. If you smoke or snort coke there can't be an infection problem with HIV or hepatitis C, right? Wrong.

'When you snort cocaine it damages the mucus membranes inside your nose, where the drug is being absorbed into the bloodstream,' said Gray. 'The more snorting you do, the more you damage the septum. When that damage is done your nose bleeds frequently. It's a classic sign of a cocaine user that they will blow their nose and produce fresh blood.

'Imagine you're at a party. There's a group of people ready to take cocaine and they're telling themselves, "This is a safe drug, it's not in the same league as, say, heroin." So there'll be someone drawing up the lines and that person will often be the first to take a snort. If he or she is a regular snorter you could have fresh blood at the end of the straw.

It's commonplace for the straw to be passed on, especially if it's in the form of a rolled-up banknote. There's some stupid thing about trust, about passing the note around the group.

'If there's another regular in the group then the chances are there'll be fresh blood to fresh blood contact. Hepatitis C, according to the latest tests from Australia, can stay alive outside the human body for up to three months. The risks are obvious. It's like sharing a needle, and of course injecting cocaine with somebody else's needle is another route for this disease to enter the body.

'The third route is smoking. People will quite often burn their fingers using a lighter. The type of crack pipe is important – some of them burn your lips or cut your mouth – and actually smoking crack cocaine dehydrates you a hell of a lot. One of the things you notice about someone emerging from a crack house is that their lips are really chapped. There's something about cocaine that makes people pick at broken skin or sores. They've got open weeping wounds on their mouths and they're passing around a crack pipe. Again, they can be passing on hepatitis C.

'Crack cocaine, because of the way it works on the brain, creates an incredible compulsion among users. You may know about the dangers but you ignore them. You get instances of people injecting cocaine and saying, "I don't care if it's a dirty spike; I don't care if you've got HIV. I just want my hit." That attitude is increasing. We have to wait and see what the impact will be on HIV and hepatitis C statistics among cocaine users. The tragedy is that – especially among the snorters – there are a lot of people out there unaware of the risks.'

Coke and HIV is a nagging worry for public health workers. Not just because cocaine offers the disease a route into the body but because of the biochemistry that unravels once it's there. A study by scientists at the University of California Los Angeles (published by NIDA, 15 February 2002) looked at the direct relationship between drug and virus and discovered a 'double whammy' effect.

The researchers took mice genetically bred to have no immune system and injected them with human cells. They then infected the cells with HIV, gave half the animals daily liquid injections of cocaine and the other half a saline solution. Ten days later they found that the cocaine mice had a 200-fold increase in HIV-infected cells coupled with a nine-fold decrease in CD4 T-cells: the cells HIV attacks to destroy its host's immune system. In other words, cocaine helps HIV to breed as it destroys the body's natural defence against the virus. Given that crack smoking and prostitution often go together, the implications are obvious.

Gray believes that governments and drug agencies should be doing more to identify cocaine addicts at an earlier stage in their illness. 'Part of the problem is that addicts do not come into services until they're in crisis,' he said. 'You'll see heroin users because they'll at least come in to get clean needles, and you can help them stabilize and manage their dependency. With crack and cocaine you'll usually see people only when the shit has really hit the fan, they're on the doorstep saying, "I need help and I need it now." We haven't got a lure to get them into services. We give out needles but we don't give out crack pipes. Maybe we should.'

Keeping cocaine addicts clean of the drug is now a huge industry. But while the theory of recovery is similar worldwide, the style can be worlds apart. If you're rich, boy can you enjoy therapy in style. If you're poor and readjusting in some backstreet halfway house, then humility is the word.

REHAB… AT A PRICE

One of the world's newest and most luxurious rehabilitation clinics is Promises Malibu in California's Santa Monica mountains. If you log on to its website you'll find it set in stunning gardens fringed with palm trees. There are idyllic sandy beaches, tennis courts, a swimming pool and stables (where you can, naturally, experience equine therapy), and the chance to take guided walks in the hills. Lunch is created by a gourmet chef and celebrity guests such as Charlie Sheen and Robert Downey Jr can relax in the knowledge that their needs are serviced through a one-to-one ratio of staff to clients. The bill? Around $29,000 (£20,000) per month.

Inevitably, questions are being asked in the media. Under the headline 'Is Rehab A Rip-Off?' (14 April 2002), *The Sunday Times' Style* magazine pointed out that five-star country retreats are not absolutely crucial to recovery. Especially at that price. It quoted Nick Heather, professor of alcohol and drug studies at Britain's University of Northumbria, who suggested that luxury surroundings might even be counter-productive.

'There is a mountain of evidence to show that you get equally good results from outpatient treatment for one-tenth of the cost,' said Heather. 'People abuse alcohol and drugs in a particular social environment. Getting them to sit around talking about problems and then throwing them back into their old world, full of temptations and opportunities to relapse, is not helpful.'

'Ritzy rehab supporters argue that the clinics carry huge staff overheads and compare favourably in price with, say, a private heart bypass operation. Robin Lefever, a former addict who runs the £12,000-per-month ($17,500) Promis Recovery Centre in Kent, England, told *The Sunday Times*, 'I make no apology for it. I believe that your surroundings have an impact on the quality of your recovery. I know what it's like to come out of detox and be sent to a really grim halfway house: it's incredibly hard. Being relaxed and having time and the right atmosphere to think in is incredibly important.'

Perhaps both sides are right. All addicts are not the same and if you're a Hollywood superstar you might feel reluctant to shuffle along to Joe Public's group therapy session if there's a chance that fellow addicts will phone the press faster than you can say celebrity coke-head. 'Private hospitals have their place,' says Aidan Gray, 'though personally I think there's an assumption from richer users that because they're paying £2,000 ($2,900) a week they're getting the best service, which isn't true. In a way it doesn't matter. A big element in recovery is belief and if paying money allows you to have more faith in the process then why not?'

THE MONEY LAUNDRY

Imagine you're a drugs baron, running cocaine from Colombia to wholesalers and street dealers in north-east America. You've contracted-out the smuggling and transport business to a Mexican cartel, which gets to keep a third of all consignments as payment. You've bribed a few police chiefs and politicians along the way and you've settled the pittance you pay coca growers. You're share is still $1 million (£700,000) a day in profit. But there's a problem.

All your income is in cash: small denominations handed over by cocaine users. The USA, along with most major western economies, insists that banks report any cash deposit of more than $10,000 (£7,000) under a process called Currency Transaction Reporting (CTR). Given that, according to the US Customs Service website (March 2002), the total American narcotics market is worth $57 billion (£39 billion) a year, and there are around 255 banking days per year, this would mean drug dealers depositing around $223.5 million (£154.2 million) per day. Even if depositors managed to make three drops a day without raising eyebrows, there would need to be 7,450 of them on the combined payroll. This is not the way drugs barons like to do business. It would be a turkey shoot for the DEA.

Depositing drug profits like this sounds farcical but, actually, isn't. When the cocaine boom hit America - and specifically Florida - in the late 1970s, US Treasury officials discovered an anomaly in their sums. Why was the Miami Federal Reserve Bank reporting a cash surplus of $5.5 billion (£3.8 billion) in 1979 - more than the surplus of the other 12 Federal Reserve Banks put together? The answer wasn't long coming. All over the state, Colombian couriers were handing in dollar bills by the bagful. Some even turned up carrying cash in supermarket trolleys.

The Bank Secrecy Act (which enforced CTR) temporarily halted this practice. Then DEA agents began reporting a curious new phenomenon in which dozens of cash couriers, each carrying amounts not dissimilar to $9,999 (£6,999), were being bussed around the banks on a daily basis. They looked so like caricatures - queuing to get off the bus, queuing to get in the banks, shoulder bags full to bursting - that the DEA nicknamed them after those much-loved cartoon characters, the Smurfs. To this day, 'smurfing' is the DEA's technical term for multiple deposits of drug money.

There are dozens of methods used to launder cash but they all involve three essential steps:

- getting the money into commercial financial systems,

either through a bank or front company
- 'layering' that cash by moving it to different accounts (so obscuring the original source)
- pumping it back into the economy as 'clean' money.

In theory, the simplest way is simply to export drug dollars in bulk to a country where banks have no CTR. The problem here is that $1 million (£700,000) in small denominations is not easy to conceal. Customs officers deploy the same techniques as in detecting drug trafficking, even training sniffer dogs to recognize the smell of money. Latest DEA figures show a doubling of currency seizures (up to $12 million/£8.3 million at a time) from $38 million (£26 million) in 1995 to $77 million (£53 million) in 1998.

Given the risks associated with bulk shipments, some cartels set up legitimate businesses as cover. Flea markets and restaurants deal in bucketloads of cash and their legal earnings can easily be pumped up with cocaine money. Front or 'shell' companies (those that are registered but don't trade) are also popular, masquerading as art dealerships, precious-metal brokers, real estate, hotel and restaurant businesses or construction companies. Fake charities and even religious organizations have been used as dirty-money conduits and you could always buy a bank or corrupt its officials. But of all the methods employed by the cocaine cartels one stands out as a perennial favourite. It is the BMPE: the Black Market Peso Exchange.

According to the US Customs Service it works like this.

- Colombian drugs bosses export their cocaine and sell it to wholesale dealers for US dollars;
- They call in a Colombian-based money changer or 'peso broker', who agrees to exchange pesos he owns in Colombia for dollar bills owned by the cartel in America;
- The cartel has now laundered its profits into 'clean' pesos and can get on with the business of trafficking cocaine;
- The peso broker meanwhile uses American contacts to channel his drug dollars into the US banking system (some or all of the above methods will be used);
- Colombian importers seeking to buy US goods and commodities place orders through the peso broker. He again uses his American associates to make the purchases, paying with the drug money now nestling in legitimate bank accounts;
- Purchased goods – typically hi-fis and TVs, household appliances, alcohol and tobacco – are exported via Europe or the Caribbean, and then smuggled into Colombia, often through the Panama Canal free trade zone. The Colombian buyer avoids hefty state import tariffs and pays the broker in pesos. The broker, who has by now charged both cartel and importer for his services, then has more pesos to buy drug dollars.

So why is this a government problem? Black markets exist everywhere – not just in Latin America – and still life goes on. The answer lies both in the fragile state of developing economies, such as Mexico, Colombia, Peru and Bolivia, and in the astonishing amount of dirty currency swilling around the system. This is money that can't be taxed, buying goods that officially don't exist and paying wages that can't be traced. You don't need to be John Maynard Keynes to realise it's bad news for national treasuries.

INVISIBLE EARNINGS

Take Mexico, for example. In 1997, before the recent government offensive against cocaine cartels, its drugs trade was worth $30 billion (£20 billion) a year: that's the equivalent of the rest of the country's gross national product (GNP) put together. The second biggest earner was the oil industry, which managed a mere $10 billion (£7 billion). By coincidence, $10 billion (£7 billion) was then the annual personal income of the drugs baron Amado Carrillo Fuentes who, you'll recall, died undergoing plastic surgery in July that same year (London *Daily Telegraph*, 18 October 1997).

Among the $800 million (£550 million) per year handed out in bribes was the purchase of unfettered air access for Carrillo's drug planes. According to one contemporary legend he would take an hour-long 'window' in Mexico's air-defence network and use it to fly through as many planes as he could, including a cocaine-laden Boeing 727. No wonder his nickname was Lord of the Skies.

Carrillo knew that his earnings were effectively keeping the Mexican economy afloat. He said as much in a letter to President Ernesto Zedillo dated 14 January 1997, which was later leaked to the press. 'Leave me alone to run my business,' it warned, 'otherwise I'll withdraw its benefits from the nation.'

US Customs officer Dean Boyd, who specializes in analyzing drug dollar laundering, believes Latin America is slowly accepting the need to challenge the economic muscle of the cartels. The BMPE, he says, acts like a parasite on a nation's wealth.

'This scam has been in place for decades; in fact, it pre-dates the drug trade altogether,' he told me. 'It is just about the largest money-laundering system in the western hemisphere and primarily sucks in Colombia, Panama, Venezuela and the United States. The only way to tackle it is for these countries to act together using every agency at their disposal. Our best estimates suggest that BMPE alone launders between $3 and $6 billion (£2 and 4 billion) every year.

'Colombia is well aware of the problem and has been for a long time because it directly affects that country's economy. It results in a huge quantity of lost tax revenue for them because, in effect, goods are smuggled in as contraband and no import taxes are paid. This has had a devastating effect on their treasury and they have really stepped up their efforts to stop it. It isn't easy because a lot of the goods go through the Panamanian free-trade zone. That can be hard to police. It is in the interests of the United States to help them because the end result is that our companies get paid in drug money. Nobody wants that.'

There is certainly plenty of US help.

OPERATION WIRE CUTTER

In September 1999 the 'El Dorado' multi-agency task force in New York launched an ambitious strike against Colombian money brokers with Operation Wire Cutter. This saw undercover Customs officers posing as American-based money launderers to penetrate the Caracol cartel on Colombia's north coast. Over several months they picked up drug dollars in cities such as New York, Miami, Chicago, Los Angeles and San Juan, Puerto Rico, wiring the cash to accounts specified by the brokers. As the net grew bigger both the DEA and Colombia's equivalent, the Departamento Administrativo de Seguridad (DAS), were called in to monitor the dirty money emerging as 'clean' pesos and then as smuggled goods in Colombia.

On 15 January 2002, the DAS arrested eight brokers in Bogotá to face currency charges in New York. Between them they had 50 years' experience in the money-laundering business and allegedly offered their services on a contract basis to several different cartels. More than

$8 million (£5.5 million) in cash and 400kg (880lbs) of cocaine was recovered. A further 29 people were held in various US cities (according to a USCS press release).

In a press statement released later, DEA administrator ASA Hutchinson said, 'By integrating electronic surveillance with investigative intelligence, US and Colombian officials tracked millions of dollars laundered through the Black Market Peso Exchange and arrested the principal money launderers involved in the conspiracy.' Colombia's US ambassador was equally chipper, describing the operation as 'a model for how other nations around the world will have to work together if we are going to be successful in shutting down global narco-trafficking and terrorist networks.'

Wire Cutter was a major coup, although no one is pretending that it will deter the cartels for long. 'All we can do is make it as difficult as possible for them to use the BMPE system,' says Dean Boyd. 'What's amazing is that the traffickers are prepared to lose so much of their profits to these brokers. If I'm a cartel boss down in Colombia and I have $10 million (£7 million) sitting in New York I'll happily sell that for $8 million (£5.5 million) worth of pesos.

'That's indicative of how lucrative the whole business is. If we can make the cost of laundering more and more expensive then we are getting somewhere. Part of our job is to make life difficult for these people and if we can make them try another system then that's a victory. One thing is for sure. Whatever else they do, they always want to get their hands on the money.

'Typically, when we mount a major operation to disrupt money laundering they go back to bulk cash smuggling. That is a risky situation for them. Carrying millions of dollars in cash weighs a lot; it's very unwieldy, difficult to transport covertly and our sniffer dogs are trained to find it. After we complete an operation we alert our people on the borders to expect more cash smuggling and, sure enough, it always happens.'

In Europe the system works in exactly the same way, with drug money converted into various national currencies and cleansed through the purchase and smuggling of black-market goods. Life may prove harder for the money launderers in future because the introduction (and inevitable adoption) of the euro as a European-wide currency will make wire transfers more transparent. Until that time comes there's always Liechtenstein as a safe haven for dodgy money.

HAVEN IN THE HILLS

This little Alpine statelet has long been famous for its secretive banking, lax regulation and negligible tax regime. That's why crooks such as the disgraced (now deceased) British publisher Robert Maxwell liked doing business there. But in January 2000 a report by Germany's Federal Intelligence Service (FIS) painted an alarming picture of the extent to which the 160 sq km (62 sq mile) principality has courted mafia bosses and drug barons, including our old friend Pablo Escobar. Through its 'cyber-spying' division, the Bundesnach- richtendienst (BND), the FIS claimed it had hard evidence that underworld figures across the world had been tapped up by men in suits from Liechtenstein.

It described meetings with the 'financial managers of South American drug clans' over many years and highlighted 'a network of relationships between high-ranking officials, judges, politicians, bank managers and investment advisers, who assist each other with illegal financial transactions on behalf of international criminals.' The German news magazine *Der Spiegel* was rather more blunt: 'The secret document reads like the worst nightmare,' it fumed. 'An entire country in the middle of Europe appears to be in the service of criminals from all around the world. The findings destroy once and for all what was left of Liechtenstein's battered reputation.'

It should be said that in the wacky world of drug money, Liechtenstein doesn't have a monopoly on battered reputations. For all its talk of consensus and multinational approaches, the White House has an undistinguished record of playing fast and loose.

PANAMA SPAT

The politics of cocaine never fail to dog the US when it blunders into South America. In Panama, their bête noire was one Manuel Noriega, a particularly loathsome bully who had been protected from child rape charges to rise to the top of the Panamanian armed forces. Panama had a reputation as a drug smuggling and money-laundering centre, but the Americans tolerated Noriega because he seemed to be on the right side. After all, Panama was acting as a pipeline for Contra guns...

Noriega was playing a dangerous game. He allowed Colombia's Medellín cartel to build a huge cocaine laboratory in the Darien jungle, accepting something between $2 and $5 million (£1.4 and £3.5 million) in bribes. He also permitted the cartel to channel coke through Panama on payment of a $1,000 (£700) per kilogram (2¼lb) tax. Things started to go wrong when Panamanian army officers heard whispers about the Darien laboratory and staged a major raid to shut it down. The Medellín bosses are rumoured to have responded by sending Noriega a gift-wrapped coffin. The White House was more restrained but began to see clearly the monster it had helped to create.

As the 1980s rolled on, Noriega lost the plot completely. He had his main political opponent assassinated for publicizing the drug deals. He was accused by his second-in-command, General Robert Diaz, of stuffing ballot boxes to secure re-election. Stupidly, he began targeting US citizens in Panama as suspected illegal aliens. And, really stupidly, he hinted that American access to the Panama Canal might not be guaranteed.

By the time Panamanians began street protests demanding Noriega's removal, Washington was on the case. On Wednesday 20 December 1989, the US military launched

Operation Just Cause against a man Senator Jesse Helms described as 'the biggest head of the biggest drug-trafficking operation in the western hemisphere'. More than 24,000 airborne US troops invaded Panama with the intention of bringing back Noriega to stand trial in Florida. Unfortunately, they couldn't find him straight away because he was busy in a brothel in Tocumen.

Soon after the invasion, Noriega tipped up at the offices of the papal ambassador in Panama City demanding sanctuary courtesy of the Catholic Church. The building was surrounded by US Special Forces, who spent a sleepless festive season blitzing the building with loud pop music. Noriega emerged on 3 January 1990 and was brought to Florida for trial. He was found guilty and will remain in jail for the foreseeable future.

You might think the lessons of Panama and Nicaragua would deter the White House from dabbling further in cocaine politics. You'd be wrong. The big three coca countries – Colombia, Peru and Bolivia – are all taking Uncle Sam's dollar as an incentive to restrict cocaine production. The hard statistics trotted out by the White House ONDCP seem encouraging.

LIES, DAMNED LIES AND ...
On 22 January 2001, ONDCP director Edward Jurith revealed that coca production had dropped 33 per cent in Bolivia and 12 per cent in Peru over the previous 12 months.

Over five years the harvest was down even more dramatically: from 94,400ha (233,200 acres) to 34,200ha (84,500 acres) in Peru and from 48,100ha (118,800 acres) to 14,600ha (36,100 acres) in Bolivia. At a press conference, Jurith presented this as a major victory.

'Bolivia and Peru have demonstrated a sustained commitment to counter-drug efforts,' he said. 'Their ability to sharply reduce coca cultivation illustrates that a long-term commitment and a solid strategy bring positive results. We look forward to continuing to work with their governments towards further reducing illicit coca production. These successes underscore that when political will is combined with comprehensive alternative economic development and the rule of law, drug cultivation and production will plummet. This is also our objective in Colombia, where Plan Colombia envisions a 50 per cent reduction in coca cultivation in five years.'

Sounds like bad news for the cartels, doesn't it? America taking the war on drugs to the enemy; being proactive instead of reactive; preventing a white wave of cocaine from breaking over its people. Doing something must surely be better than doing nothing, right? Let's probe Jurith's statement a little further. Let's start with 'Plan Colombia'...

This is a $1.3 billion (£0.9 million) military package introduced in 2000 by President Clinton to help the Colombian army destroy illegal coca plantations, fight cocaine trafficking and target rebel guerrillas in the country's heartlands. Over two years the Americans have provided more than 100 Black Hawk and Huey 2 helicopters, and hundreds of US troops acting as trainers and advisers. This intervention was a bold policy, which the European Union and most of South America refused to back.

European leaders were concerned that Colombia's appalling record on human rights had not been addressed. The 12 South American presidents (some of whom represented nations with equally grim records), meanwhile, reckoned that Plan Colombia missed the point altogether. At their August 2000 summit in Brasilia they argued that the USA should reduce market demand for cocaine, restrict the chemicals used in its production and do more to help peasant farmers grow different crops. Venezuela, Ecuador, Peru and Brazil all tightened security along their borders with Colombia, fearing a refugee crisis and a spill-over of military action.

In February 2001 the US Army delivered an interim report claiming that the coca destruction programme was going swimmingly. Nearly a quarter of Colombia's plantations had been destroyed in two months of aerial fumigation. However, commanders were cagey about the remaining three-quarters, most of which are in jungle territory controlled by the powerful left-wing guerrilla group FARC (the Revolutionary Armed Forces of Colombia).

Since 1999, FARC has effectively governed a 3.8 million ha (9.4 million acres) 'de-militarized zone', offered by President Andres Pastrana in a desperate attempt to end the country's debilitating civil war. Known unofficially as Farclandia, the world's newest nation, it includes some of Latin America's most productive coca plantations. The problem for the USA is that FARC fills its war chest with drug money. It taxes paste makers and has set itself up as a monopoly buyer of coca leaf.

According to *The Sunday Telegraph* (3 September 2000), FARC earns around £600 million ($870 million) a year from cocaine. It controls 70 per cent of the coca fields and sets the price (around £700/$1,000 per kilo/2¼lb of leaf). Although it has other methods of fundraising – Farclandia law 002 states that anyone worth more than $1 million (£700,000) must hand over 10 per cent for the rebel cause – it needs the drug trade for its political ambitions. It is unlikely that American crop-eradication helicopters will be invited in to spray a genetically modified anti-coca fungus. As General Fernando Tapias, head of the Colombian armed forces, told the newpaper: 'There will be peace. But first there will be war.'

FARC is not the only player in Colombia's coca market. Its sworn enemy, not counting the government, is the Self-Defence Forces of Colombia (AUC), which controls some 7,000 right-wing paramilitaries based around the bustling market town of Puerto Asis. This is also good coca country, with around 60,000ha (148,000 acres) devoted to the leaf. Predictably, the AUC is equally cautious about its cash crop being zapped by US chemical sprayers. According to one peasant farmer in the region, Jose Sonza, 'the paras [AUC] are offering 2.4 million pesos [£800/$1,160] for a kilo of coca base whilst the guerrillas in the jungle [FARC] only pay 1.8 million [£600/$870]' (London *Daily Telegraph*, 24 August 2000).

The reality is that Plan Colombia may actually be fuelling coca production and cocaine prices elsewhere. On 17 February 2001, the British Broadcasting Corporation (BBC) carried a report on its website that began, 'Fears are growing that Peru could soon regain its title of being the world's number one cocaine supplier. It is because of the huge US-financed anti-drugs operation in neighbouring Colombia.'

This report went on to reveal that new coca fields had been sighted in south-east Peru. It quoted the UN Drug Control Programme representative, Patricio Vandenberghe, who predicted that a shift in coca production from Colombia to its neighbours was a 'logical move'. A UN investigator, Humberto Chirrinos, said Peruvian farmers were being lured back to the industry as leaf prices rose 100 per cent: from $2 (£1.40) to $4 (£2.80) per kilogram (21/4lb) over the second half of 2000. This is basic economic stuff. Restrict supply of a desirable commodity and – everything else being equal – buyers will pay more.

AN UNWORKABLE SOLUTION
As the world's 'boilerhouse' economy, the United States knows all about wealth. What's not so clear is whether Jurith

and the White House have got to grips with the politics of poverty. The idea that all South American coca farmers can switch seamlessly to new crops subsidized by US dollars is not credible.

Sanho Tree is a fellow of the Institute of Policy Studies (IPS), a respected Washington DC think-tank that prides itself on 'unconventional wisdom to public policy problems'. Tree heads the IPS's Drug Policy Project. He is scathing about White House claims of success in the coca fields.

'The eradication programme is absolute folly,' he told me. 'It doesn't take into account how much land there is for potential cultivation, nor does it appreciate the reserve army of the poor, the people who are prepared to defy the US and take a risk on growing coca.

'The bureaucrats are concerned only with Congressional mandates such as how many hectares have been eradicated in a year. They can't see that crop eradication is actually a great form of price subsidy. It takes a lot of coca off the market and ensures a high price for everything that's left. This is essentially what we're doing when we pay American farmers not to farm legal crops such as soya beans and maize.

'In countries like Bolivia, eradication has had a quite brutal effect on local people. This is because no money or thought is put into alternative development – or indeed any basic development. Bolivia is the poorest country in Latin America and it is now suffering great social upheaval.

'We have taken a relatively peaceful country and pushed it to the brink of civil war. Civil war isn't quite the right description because one side is well armed and the other has virtually nothing. But the *campesinos* [coca farmers] are now starting to ask, "Where can we get guns, we can't take this any more." They've tried peaceful protests, they've been shot at, they've been killed, and they are told to go and grow other crops that no one wants.

'The idea has been an utter failure. The United States asks peasant coca farmers to switch to fruit, which they must transport in vehicles they don't have, down roads that don't exist, to sell in markets with no buyers. Even if there were customers the idea that the *campesinos* could compete in an international global economy is truly farcical. They wouldn't stand a chance.'

But peasant farmers are not all angels. They are allowed to grow coca for 'traditional use' and the White House is surely right to suspect that some of it reaches paste makers for conversion into cocaine. Again, Tree is unconvinced.

'Even if some legally grown coca is ending up in illegal markets – and I don't see much evidence yet for this – getting rid of it is not going to make any difference,' he said. 'Certainly not in terms of reducing street cocaine in the USA, which is ostensibly what eradication is supposed to be all about. Colombia's output is more than adequate to make up the difference and in Peru they're already replanting. The whole policy is a horrible failure.

'In Colombia FARC is now forcing farmers to grow coca whether they want to or not. Our interference there is actually helping to increase cultivation. FARC will fund their war no matter what it takes. They don't have a choice. I'm really not sure what the US government expects here.

'There is growing alarm in Congress about the transition from a counter-narcotics mission in Colombia to counter-insurgency and now to counter-terrorism. A lot of Congressmen are prepared to go along with the global war on terror because they're afraid to oppose it. But it is worrying that both parties, the Clinton administration, and even the Bush administration until recently, had promised the American people: "Don't worry, we're not getting sucked into this four-decade-old civil war. We're just fighting drugs." And now suddenly we're protecting an oil pipeline and we're fighting guerrillas and we're not looking at mission creep* any more, we're looking at mission gallop.'

Kathryn Ledebur agrees. As co-ordinator of the Andean Information Network in Cochabama she spends her time highlighting 'US folly' in Bolivia's coca fields. She says the American eradication programme – 'Plan Dignity' – has been anything but dignified since it began in 1997. Instead there has been an escalating series of conflicts, culminating in the deaths of ten coca growers and four members of the security forces between September 2001 and February 2002. More than 350 other farmers have been injured or detained.

* military term for the way in which politicians expand clear military objectives into a range of complex ones

BITTER HARVEST

'The plan has targeted the very poorest people in Bolivia, the peasant farmers who grow coca leaf for survival,' said Ledebur. 'It doesn't significantly attack high-level drug traffickers or money launderers. The Bolivian government has eradicated huge amounts of coca in the Chapare [one of the main growing regions] but promises of alternative crops and employment are proving slow to deliver. As a result, levels of poverty and malnutrition in an already poor tropical region have soared.

'This is the first time the Bolivian military has ever taken a role in anti-drug operations. We have a country that has been democratic for less than 25 years and, at a time when we should be strengthening that democracy, we are instead creating strong, well-funded roles for the Bolivian military. There are conscripts who have to pull up the coca and there's a huge military police presence in the Chapare. This has led to a series of violent conflicts, many involving the so-called Expeditionary Task Force, which is a very strange group funded almost exclusively by the USA. These people are non-military; they are hired hands working under military command and they have been implicated in some of the most serious human rights violations to have occurred.

'It is true that nothing will be able to replace the income from coca in the Chapare but, as stipulated by the law, there needs to be something that provides an income for 35,000 families. What we've seen by aggressive US eradication is that they have pushed coca production around the Andean region. You have these big advances in Bolivia – it's heralded as the great anti-drug success – and yet Colombia is easily filling the gap in the market and Peru is planting again. We're actually seeing a net increase in the amount of coca grown and no noticeable impact on the price, purity and availability of cocaine on American streets.

'There is going to be a permanently funded US military presence in the Chapare. It will cost $10,000 (£6,900) a day to keep this force and that's roughly the cost of building a school. There is no exit strategy here. The farmers have no alternative, so they replant coca leaf. Governments say that justifies a military presence. The coca gets pulled up by the military, the farmers replant and so the cycle goes on.'

These views are echoed by peasant farmers across the Chapare. One, Zenon Cruz, told the London Guardian (25 August 2000) how he had been forced to grow beans and oranges instead of coca. Plan Dignity meant that he and his family had to live on a fraction of their former income. 'My father sowed coca and his father sowed it before him,' he said. 'What the Americans do not understand is that this leaf is a gift from mother earth to our people, an ancient tradition. They do not understand its sacredness. They think it is all about drugs.'

More pragmatically, he added, 'You can fill a lorry with oranges and not sell any of them at market. But coca always sells like hot bread. I was making 150 bolivianos [about £20/$29] a week before they cut down the coca. Now we sometimes struggle to make 20 [£3/$4.50]. How can you feed a family on that?'

Another farmer, Celestino Quispe, was interviewed by BBC news in La Paz in June 2000. Reading his words you can't help but question the standard western government propaganda that brands everything about the drugs business evil. Quispe patently isn't evil. Like most parents, he's just trying to do his best for his kids.

'Coca is a means of survival for us,' he said. 'Because the soil is very tired, very eroded. Coca leaves are the only option we have for earning a living to feed ourselves and our families. We can't substitute it with other products like citrus fruits or coffee. Citrus fruits are very cheap. There are supplies sitting there rotting. I would not be able to feed my family by growing citrus fruits.

'Coffee is annual, whereas I can harvest coca leaves three times a year. It does go down in price sometimes, but we always manage with coca. True, we have to replant every five or six years because the soil has to be renovated. But we can earn a living. You get much more money from coca leaves than you do for oranges. It's a very big difference in price. And oranges are heavy, so by the time you've paid for the transport to get them to the market there is nothing left for the producer.

'I have five children. Coca leaves allow me to pay for

their education. My children are able to study, which I was not. I have little choice in what I can do for a living now but I am trying to make sure that they get qualifications. I would like for them to be able to choose what they want to do in the future. An education is very important because it will give them choice: they will be able to decide whether they want to grow coca like me or do something different, something better.

'Also, remember that coca leaves are not all bad. They are not only used to feed a habit. Coca leaves are also medicinal and a source of a traditional, legal beverage. There are no *cocalero* [coca grower] drug addicts. It is the gringos who have processed the coca leaves with chemical products as a drug.'

This is the argument now being drummed into a new generation of Indians. When families in Bolivia's fertile Yungas valleys gather to make their traditional offering to Pachamama, the earth goddess, they sprinkle coca leaves and alcohol on the ground next to burning incense. Their children then sing in Quechua:

> *Green coca you are born of our land*
> *Your fragrance makes us sing happily*
> *In the fields among the mountains*
> *My little coca leaf is sweet medicine*
> *Not a drug that does damage*
> *We suck your juices for help in our work*

For the poorest of rural Indian families, coca offers comfort in a harsh world. The irony is that their much-loved leaf – worth so much in the world's wealthiest nation – has never, and will never, rescue them from poverty. That's the sad thing about the cocaine business. The few who get rich are ruthless murdering bastards. Most of the rest stay poor.

BROKE ON COKE

Here's some food for thought. In 1969 the White House ONDCP spent $0.65 billion (£0.45 billion). By 1981, Ronald Reagan's first year as president, this had risen to $1 billion (£0.7 billion). In 1999, under Bill Clinton, it had reached $17.1 billion (£11.8 billion). This is serious money even by US Treasury standards. And still, every 30 seconds, someone in America is arrested on drug charges.

One in five inmates in a prison is there for a drug offence. Almost two out of three Federal prisoners are serving time for drugs. The total annual cost of keeping drug violators locked up is around $8.6 billion (£6 billion). Counting the ONDCP budget, that adds up to $25.7 billion (£17.7 billion) a year to 'control' drug use. God alone knows how much this increases if you factor in time spent by police, DEA, US Customs, the Coast Guard, Army, Navy, Air Force and assorted ranks of government bureaucrats. If you were running America would you call this drug control? Only if you were as high as a space cadet. (The above statistics were cited in *The Social Impact Of Drugs And The War On Drugs*, Professor Craig Reinarman, IPS May 1999)

Now relax. We are not about to plunge into the dreaded quicksand of social science. Besides, any argument that there's some neat and squeaky-clean answer to recreational drug use is absurd. No country has ever won a war on drugs, except accidentally when it happened to be fighting a proper war at the time. Even then success proved to be short-lived. As for decriminalization...no, I can sense you glazing over. However, cocaine's relationship with crime, poverty and – especially – racism in the USA is interesting. We know how scare stories of the early 20th century shaped hysterical legislation (remember the indestructible 'cocaine nigger'), but what's really scary is the way US courts still see poor, black, crack cocaine users as more deserving of harsh punishment than rich, white powder cokers. Scarier still is the view among many black community leaders that this strategy is right.

In the USA, sentences in crack cases are far longer than those for powder-coke offences. Smuggling or dealing 100g (3½oz) of powder attracts the same penalty as an offence involving just 1g of crack (cited, again, in Prof Reinarman's report). Why so? It's the same drug. Crack is more popular in poor neighbourhoods (because it's cheap), but you can't start banging people up for longer just because their drug of choice happens to be popular. On that basis just about every American citizen would end up doing 12 years for marijuana offences. There is an argument that crack is more addictive, and more likely to provoke street crime, but then converting powder to crack is a cinch anyway.

Dr David Smith at Haight-Ashbury Free Clinic (HAFC) in San Francisco despairs of the 'lock 'em up' fraternity. 'I have found that politicians and public officials are often wrong but never in doubt,' he says. 'They will stand up and say, "You can't treat crack-cocaine addiction. That's why we have to put them in jail." Well, actually, we have large numbers of successes with crack cocaine.

'Early intervention is the key. If you criminalize the drug, then this becomes so much harder. You can't tell some politicians that because they just want to lock up all the drug addicts. We are talking penny wise pound foolish here. If as a society we don't pay straight away we will surely pay later.

'We have a fundamentally racist system in that we put all the black crack addicts in jail and all the white cocaine addicts in treatment centres. There's been an increased government emphasis on criminalization and a decreased emphasis on early-intervention programmes such as at HAFC. I actually don't include San Francisco in this because we're almost a different country as far as drug treatment goes. We have a much broader base of support for our efforts.

'Europe needs to learn from America's experience. We need to share this globally and understand the dynamics of drug culture. There is so much uninformed opinion that serves as a basis for policy. These epidemics and why they happen and what we can do about them: this all needs to be studied in an objective, professional manner.'

CLASS DISTINCTION

In May 1999 the Institute for Policy Studies looked at the class-and-crack issue as part of its Citizens Commission on US Drug Policy, held in Los Angeles. These hearings brought together senior judges, law professors and prison reformers to take evidence from experts. One of the witnesses was Franklin Ferguson Jr, a black civil-rights attorney.

'This problem begins not with race but with class,' he said. 'Like a range of other crimes past and present the drug trade consists of consensual transactions that take place within organized sales and distribution networks. These networks tend to segment by economic class. The rise of crack in the 1980s produced a class divide in the cocaine market that was unusually visible.'

He then listed the 'retributive' factors that have persuaded judges in cocaine cases to be tougher on poor crack smokers and dealers than they are on rich powder snorters and dealers.

'The former are certainly perceived to cause greater social harm than the latter and therefore seem to deserve harsher treatment,' he said. 'Lower-class criminal markets tend to be more violent than their upper-class equivalents, at least in terms of the manner in which our society typically measures violence. It is easier to catch and punish sellers and buyers in lower-class markets than it is to catch and punish their higher-end, white-collar counterparts. The lower-class markets are eminently more visible. Lower-class constituents simply possess a much lower expectation of privacy, in direct proportion to their possession of land and property. This does not, however, justify the practice.

'Many have come to believe that because whites disproportionately use powder cocaine while blacks disproportionately use crack cocaine, a two-tier system of punishment has developed. The disparity between the amount of powder cocaine and crack cocaine required to warrant the same penalty for drug trafficking is 100 to 1.'

Ferguson quoted figures showing how the legal system's crusade against crack had significantly increased the proportion of black prisoners in US jails. In 1997 the prison population was estimated at 1,725,842, 51 per cent of whom were African-Americans. Yet African-Americans made up just 13 per cent of the total US population.

Of the 2,100 federal prisoners doing time in jail for crack, 92 per cent were African-American, compared to just 27 per cent of the 5,800 federal prisoners sentenced for powder coke. Finally there's the 'killer' fact that sentences in crack cases 'average three to eight times longer than sentences for comparable powder offenders'.

In his evidence Ferguson said, 'Even amongst staunch advocates of the black urban poor community there is support for this apparent disparity in enforcement. The crack trade destroys not only those who engage in it but also the neighbourhoods in which it takes place. Those neighbourhoods are filled with predominantly honourable black citizens who do not buy and sell crack. These citizens...may benefit from sentencing and enforcement policies that target crack relative to other drugs since crack's residual, often violent, criminal activities are simultaneously targeted.'

In other words most black people living in areas rife with crack dealing don't care that the majority of arrests involve other blacks. Nor do they care about hefty sentences. They just want these people run out of town.

Naturally, politicians notice this mindset. Nobody, they tell themselves, ever got kicked out of office for talking tough on drugs. Locking up crack users is easier to sell to the voters than funding new treatment centres. Crack cocaine is good for scare stories and scare stories are good for talking tough. QED: lock the bastards up.

SNOUTING OUT A SCAPEGOAT

This brand of political logic was addressed by Prof Reinarman, professor of sociology at the University of California, Santa Cruz, at the 1999 LA Citizens' Commission hearings. There he delivered a paper entitled 'The Social Construction Of Drug Scares', which among other things considered that old election chestnut: the scapegoat. Scapegoating was defined by Reinarman as 'blaming a drug or its alleged effects on a group of its users for a variety of pre-existing social ills that are typically only indirectly associated with it'. Reading his paper you realise that, with some half-decent spin doctoring, absolutely anything can be blamed on drugs.

'To listen to the Temperance crusaders,' said Reinarman, 'one might have believed that without alcohol use America would be a land of infinite economic progress with no poverty, crime, mental illness or even sex outside marriage. To listen to leaders of organized medicine and the government in the 1960s one might have surmised that without marijuana and LSD there would have been neither conflict between youth and their parents nor opposition to the Vietnam War. And to believe politicians and the media in the past six years is to believe that without the scourge of crack the inner cities and the so-called underclass would, if not disappear, at least be far less scarred by poverty, violence and crime.

'There is no historical evidence supporting any of this. In short, drugs are richly functional scapegoats. They provide élites with fig leaves to place over unsightly social ills that are endemic to the social system over which they preside. And they provide the public with a restricted aperture of attribution in which only a chemical bogeyman or the lone deviants who ingest it are seen as the cause of a cornucopia of complex problems.'

The truth is that crack cocaine is directly linked to poverty, both for those who grow it and those who take it.

But it's not the cause of crime and poverty in the ghetto any more than powder cocaine is the cause of fraud and wealth on Wall Street. The distinguished Harvard law professor Derek Curtis Bok once famously observed that 'if you think education is expensive, try ignorance'. Ignorance breeds poverty. Ignorance of cocaine breeds addiction.

COCAINE: THE NEXT HIT

Cocaine will always be with us. It's better than sex (at least, that's what it tells your brain) and about as easy to ban. Given that it can't be uninvented, expunged from the face of the earth or chemically altered to be user-friendly, the only issue is how to manage its presence. The smart-arse answer is to try anything that hasn't already proved a failure. The overall result may not be a triumph, but it is hard to see how things will be worse.

In political circles buzz phrases like 'blue sky thinking' and 'thinking outside the box' are trendy at the moment. Like all the best doctrinal clichés, they have wonderfully flexible meanings. Even so, the clear impression delivered to voters is that shibboleths are OUT, creativity is IN and no idea is off-limits. As politicians, police officers and editors raise the stakes in the war on drugs, we're seeing new initiatives taken up like nose candy at a Wall Street executive's leaving party.

Among the most radical of these ideas supported, worryingly, by both the liberal left and rabid right, is the decriminalization of 'hard' drugs. This book hasn't touched on this subject, because 'decriminalization' is an offensively bureaucratic word and the arguments for and against it are tediously polarized. The same applies to the debate on making drugs legally available over the counter. Let's get this over with quickly.

DOUBTS ABOUT DECRIMINALIZATION

The three big advantages cited in favour of legal use are:

- the market for drug trafficking would collapse;
- the police would be able to focus on other crimes;
- users could be properly monitored and educated.

Sure, a few dealers would struggle on, undercutting state prices or offering something that bit stronger. But the real drug money would be gone for good. Coke use would be up front and manageable.

Unfortunately, from what we know about cocaine, there are moral and practical problems with these arguments. For a start, who's going to decide when a crack addict has had enough crack? Certainly not the addict: he or she will want to smoke until death intervenes. Of course, you may feel that crack-heads have a right to decide to die this way. But are they really deciding? As Jodie, a former crack user puts it, 'People talk about using cocaine as a question of personal choice but, eventually, choice is denied you.'

Then there's the dilemma of younger users. Do we say coke is OK at the age of 18, 16, 14 or 12? What's wrong with a five-year-old trying it? Who decides on 'safe' purity levels? As soon as you dilute cocaine or make it off-limits to anybody you instantly create a new black market. Maybe not so big, but still there. That means more trafficking and more policemen hunting traffickers. As for making powder coke legal but continuing to proscribe crack – please, do pay attention at the back there!

BACK IN THE REAL WORLD…
Assuming that cocaine will always be with us and always be recreationally illegal, what might world governments usefully do? They could help America eradicate coca crops, making life harder for producers and traffickers. Harder, sometimes, but also more profitable (remember, destroying coca supports its market price). And not as hard as the life facing peasant farmers for whom coca is the only practical means of survival. Crop eradication as it stands is becoming more discredited by the day.

Perhaps the war on drugs could be intensified. More gunships and attack helicopters, more soldiers and armed agents, more nifty electronic surveillance, bigger rewards for informers…all could inflict serious damage on the trafficker. But not all traffickers. And when you've hit so many that cocaine supplies become scarce, up goes the price and in comes a new generation of millionaire coke kings.

There's the laughingly named deterrent factor, of course. This means locking up drug users and dealers for long stretches. It's great news for prison officers seeking job security but a real bummer for the rest of us who pay the bills. Drug users get to use more drugs in prison. Traffickers on the outside cheer loudly because the competition's out of action. As for the deterrent factor, there's not been much success there in half a century.

Finally there's that old favourite in the politician's armoury: the scare tactic. This essentially involves middle-aged, stressed-out people telling young carefree people that having fun is no good for them. All right, they can have fun reading or listening to music (quietly) but certainly not doing drugs. Alcohol doesn't count because lots of middle-aged, stressed-out people enjoy the odd drink.

Scare tactics never work in the long term. The classic response of parents to the first big wave of cocaine use that hit in the 1980s was to tell their children:

- 'You don't want to know about this';
- 'You will do yourself harm if you try it';
- 'We will do you harm if you try it'.

Funnily enough, these responses pretty much reflected US government policy. Telling young people that cocaine will either kill them or get them jailed is not a sensible plank on which to base an entire policy.

Most studies suggest something like 80 per cent of powder-coke users never report health problems. Users themselves aren't stupid. They know this. What they really need is clear, unbiased information about the true level of risk to the best of current knowledge. How much more effective would it be for governments and the mass media to put health risks into perspective. But then 'drugs', 'politics', 'media' and 'perspective' are not words that sit easily together in the same sentence.

As in most things, balance is the key. It's probably right to reduce coca crops as long as farmers are offered a realistic new living. It's right to lock up murderous traffickers and dealers, but sensible to keep addicts out of jail and in publicly funded treatment centres. It's right to stress the dangers of coke and also to accept that many users never become ill or addicted. If we are going to fight a drugs war let's at least stop truth becoming the first casualty.

Next time you're introduced to Charlie, by all means enjoy his company. But don't arrange to meet regularly. He can be so two-faced at times.

ABC OF STREET NAMES FOR COCAINE

(Note that this is not a definitive list; new street names are emerging all the time.)

Angie

Aunt Nora

Base (used for cocaine and crack)

Batman (also used for heroin)

Bazulco

Bernie's flakes

Big bloke

Big C

Bolivian marching powder

Bouncing powder

California cornflakes

Carrie

Cecil

Charlie

Cholly

Double bubble

Dream

Esnortiar (Spanish)

Everclear

Flake

Florida snow

Foo foo

Friskie powder

Gift-of-the-sun-god

Gin

Girl

Happy dust

Heaven

Her

Icing

Jejo

Jelly

King

Lady

Late night

Love affair

Mama coca

Monster

Movie star drug

Nose candy

Oyster stew

Paradise

Pearl

Pimp

Polvo blanco (Spanish)

Quill (also heroin; methamphetamine)

Ready rock (crack cocaine)

Roxanne

Scottie

She

Sleigh ride

Snow/snowbird

Speedball (cocaine/heroin mix)

Teenager

Teeth

Thing

Toot

Whizbang (cocaine/heroin mix)

Yeyo (Spanish)

Zip

GLOSSARY

Alkaloid – mind-altering nitrogen-based organic compound found in many drugs, including cocaine

Balling – vaginally implanted cocaine

Base crazies – people who search on their hands and knees for cocaine/crack

Based out – crack or freebase user unable to control usage

Beiging – chemicals that alter the appearance of cocaine to make it look as if it is of purer quality than it actually is

Bipping – snorting heroin and cocaine simultaneously

BMPE – Black Market Peso Exchange (method of laundering drug money)

Body packer – smuggler who swallows packets of cocaine

Break night – staying up all night on a cocaine binge

C joint – place where cocaine is sold

Campesinos – coca leaf farmers

Chalked up – under influence of cocaine

Chuspa – coca pouch carried by leaf chewers

CIA – America's Central Intelligence Agency

Cocaine hydrochloride – chemical name for powder coke; sometimes called cocaine salt

Cocalos – coca leaf plantations

Coke bar – pub or bar where cocaine is taken openly

Coke bugs – form of toxic psychosis in which cocaine addicts believe insects or snakes are crawling beneath their skin

Cooking up – processing powder coke into crack

Coqueros – coca chewers

Crash – feeling of dismay/depression that follows the cocaine 'high' or 'rush'

Cutting – process in which powder coke is chopped into lines using credit card or razor blade; process of diluting cocaine with other substances, eg glucose

DEA – America's Drug Enforcement Administration

Dopamine – chemical messenger in brain closely associated with euphoric feeling produced by cocaine

Drive-by shooting – popular gangland assassination technique in which the gunman opens fire from a moving car

Drug dollars – money earned through illicit drug sales

Flame cooking – smoking cocaine freebase by placing the pipe over a stove flame

Freebase – powder coke converted by chemical process to a smokable form

Gak-blowing – taking cocaine anally

Ghostbusting – searching for any white particle in the conviction that it is crack

Hash – cannabis or marijuana

High – euphoric feeling produced by cocaine

Horning – inhaling cocaine

Iscupuru – container, often a gourd, containing Ilipta, an alkaline substance (see below)

Line – powder coke laid out ready for snorting

Llipta – alkaline, such as lime or powdered shell, used to leach out alkaloids from coca leaf during chewing

Los Pistoleros – assassination technique in which the gunman sits as pillion passenger on a motorbike; the favoured method of Colombian cartels

LSD – lysergic acid diethylamide – potent hallucinatory drug

Mule – smuggler who carries drugs in the body or in luggage

Neurotransmitter – chemical messenger that allows brain cells to communicate with each other

NIDA – National Institute on Drug Abuse (US research organization)

ONDCP – Office of National Drug Control Policy (based at the White House, USA)

Paste – crudely processed cocaine, often in brick form

Reinforcer – brain mechanism that urges that an action be repeated

Reward pathway – method by which the brain decides that an action is good and should be repeated; sex, food, warmth and child-rearing have strong reward pathways – none of these is as strong as a cocaine habit

Rock – piece of crack cocaine

Rock starring – sex with a man/woman who takes crack cocaine as payment

Rush – euphoric feeling produced by cocaine

Satiety – brain mechanism that decides when an enjoyable experience should end

Septum – area between nostrils, sometimes destroyed by prolonged cocaine use

Seratonin – chemical messenger in brain linked to euphoria caused by cocaine use

Shebanging – mixing cocaine with water and spraying it up the nose

Smurfing – laundering drug money by depositing large quantities of
cash in banks

Spliff – cigarette containing crack cocaine

Stone – piece of crack cocaine

Synapses – spaces between brain nerve cells in which cocaine causes
build-up of dopamine and consequent euphoria

Taxing – process in which one drug gang robs another

Yardies – general description for Jamaican underworld gangs

COCAINE: A LINE THROUGH TIME

Prehistory: Andean Indians discover properties of coca

12th century AD: Rise of the Inca; coca established as a key element of religious life in South America

1502: Columbus expedition makes contact with coca-chewing Indians

1532: Francisco Pizarro's private army invades Peru

1546: Spanish rediscover the silver mines of Potosi; paying miners in coca leaf becomes more widespread

1552: Roman Catholic Church makes first attempt to ban the 'evil' herb coca

1609: Contemporary accounts show that the Church is getting a slice of coca profits and no longer makes a fuss

1786: French biologist Jean Chevalier de Lamarck classifies the leaf as Erythroxylum coca

1859: Research student Albert Niemann extracts the cocaine alkaloid from coca, so 'inventing' cocaine

1863: Vin Mariani – a wine containing cocaine – is launched to wide acclaim in Europe

1884: Sigmund Freud begins experiments with the drug

1884: Freud's student colleague Carl Koller discovers cocaine's use as a local anaesthetic

1884: Freud tries to cure morphine addiction in his friend Ernst von Fleischl-Marxow by administering cocaine

1885: Fleischl-Marxow becomes the world's first coke addict

1885: American John Pemberton comes up with a cocaine drink syrup he calls Coca-Cola

1905: Amid mounting public concern, the Coca-Cola company
     removes cocaine from its drink

1914: The New York Times carries reports of a 'cocaine nigger' turned
     into a crazed killer by the drug

1921: The Fatty Arbuckle scandal highlights widespread cocaine use in
     Hollywood

1922: New laws in America impose ten-year jail sentence on convicted
     cocaine dealers

WWII years: Cocaine use all but disappears in America

1949: United Nations begins process of closing legal coke
     laboratories in Peru

1950s: Cuba emerges as the centre of global cocaine trafficking

Late 1960s: Colombia begins to challenge Cuba for control of world
     markets

1970: Rolling Stone magazine declares cocaine 'Drug of the Year'

1973: Pinochet gains power in Chile; hundreds of Chilean traffickers
     extradited to America

1975: Full-scale cocaine war breaks out between rival cartels in
     Colombia

Late 1970s: Pablo Escobar emerges as Colombia's most powerful
     drugs baron

1979: Huge cocaine money-laundering operation identified in Florida

1979: US officials begin covert support for Contra rebels in
     Nicaragua; turn blind eye as drug running to America helps
     finance the war

Mid-1980s: Escobar's cocaine profits estimated at $1 million
     (£700,000) a day; number of American coke users tops ten
     million; crack cocaine becomes widespread in USA

1984: Colombian anti-drug crusader and justice minister Lara Bonilla assassinated

1986: CIA-Contra scandal exposed by US press

1989: US launches Operation Just Cause against Panama's Manuel Noriega

1992: Escobar shot dead by Colombian police

2000: President Clinton launches Plan Colombia to wipe out coca plantations in the country

2001: Jamaica highlighted as new centre for cocaine trafficking

2002: British and European press highlight crack cocaine wars among underworld gangs

2002: Coca farmers battle US-backed forces eradicating coca crops in Bolivia